W9-BLR-578

Gun Control

Other Books of Related Interest:

Opposing Viewpoints Series

Gun Violence

At Issue Series

School Shootings

"Congress shall make
no law ... abridging
the freedom of speech,
or of the press."

First Amendment to the U.S. Constitution

The basic foundation of our democracy is the First Amendment guarantee of freedom of expression. The Opposing Viewpoints Series is dedicated to the concept of this basic freedom and the idea that it is more important to practice it than to enshrine it.

OPPOSING VIEWPOINTS® SERIES

Gun Control

Tamara L. Roleff, Book Editor

GREENHAVEN PRESS
An imprint of Thomson Gale, a part of The Thomson Corporation

Detroit • New York • San Francisco • New Haven, Conn. • Waterville, Maine • London

Christine Nasso, *Publisher*
Elizabeth Des Chenes, *Managing Editor*

© 2007 Thomson Gale, a part of The Thomson Corporation.

Thomson and Star logo are trademarks and Gale and Greenhaven Press are registered trademarks used herein under license.

For more information, contact:
Greenhaven Press
27500 Drake Rd.
Farmington Hills, MI 48331-3535
Or you can visit our Internet site at http://www.gale.com

Articles in Greenhaven Press anthologies are often edited for length to meet page requirements. In addition, original titles of these works are changed to clearly present the main thesis and to explicitly indicate the author's opinion. Every effort is made to ensure that Greenhaven Press accurately reflects the original intent of the authors. Every effort has been made to trace the owners of copyrighted material.

Cover photograph reproduced by permission of freephotos.com.

LIBRARY OF CONGRESS CATALOGING-IN-PUBLICATION DATA

Gun control / Tamara L. Roleff, book editor.
   p. cm. -- (Opposing viewpoints)
   Includes bibliographical references and index.
   ISBN-13: 978-0-7377-3660-1 (hardcover)
   ISBN-13: 978-0-7377-3661-8 (pbk.)
   1. Firearms--Law and legislation--United States. 2. Firearms ownership--United States. 3. Gun control--United States. I. Roleff, Tamara L., 1959-
   KF3942.H3G86 2007
   344.7305'33--dc22
                             2007005374

ISBN-10: 0-7377-3660-7 (hardcover)
ISBN-10: 0-7377-3661-5 (pbk.)

Printed in the United States of America
10 9 8 7 6 5 4 3 2 1

Contents

Chapter 1: Is Gun Ownership a Threat to Society?

Chapter 2: Does the Second Amendment Protect Private Gun Ownership?

Chapter 3: Do Gun Control Regulations Reduce Crime and Violence?

Chapter 4: What Measures Would Reduce Gun Violence?

Why Consider
Opposing Viewpoints?

> *"The only way in which a human be-
> ing can make some approach to know-
> ing the whole of a subject is by hearing
> what can be said about it by persons of
> every variety of opinion and studying all
> modes in which it can be looked at by
> every character of mind. No wise man
> ever acquired his wisdom in any mode
> but this."*
>
> *John Stuart Mill*

In our media-intensive culture it is not difficult to find differing opinions. Thousands of newspapers and magazines
and dozens of radio and television talk shows resound with
differing points of view. The difficulty lies in deciding which
opinion to agree with and which "experts" seem the most
credible. The more inundated we become with differing opinions and claims, the more essential it is to hone critical reading and thinking skills to evaluate these ideas. Opposing Viewpoints books address this problem directly by presenting
stimulating debates that can be used to enhance and teach
these skills. The varied opinions contained in each book examine many different aspects of a single issue. While examining these conveniently edited opposing views, readers can de-
velop critical thinking skills such as the ability to compare and
contrast authors' credibility, facts, argumentation styles, use of
persuasive techniques, and other stylistic tools. In short, the
Opposing Viewpoints series is an ideal way to attain the
higher-level thinking and reading skills so essential in a culture of diverse and contradictory opinions.

In addition to providing a tool for critical thinking, Opposing Viewpoints books challenge readers to question their own strongly held opinions and assumptions. Most people form their opinions on the basis of upbringing, peer pressure, and personal, cultural, or professional bias. By reading carefully balanced opposing views, readers must directly confront new ideas as well as the opinions of those with whom they disagree. This is not to simplistically argue that everyone who reads opposing views will—or should—change his or her opinion. Instead, the series enhances readers' understanding of their own views by encouraging confrontation with opposing ideas. Careful examination of others' views can lead to the readers' understanding of the logical inconsistencies in their own opinions, perspective on why they hold an opinion, and the consideration of the possibility that their opinion requires further evaluation.

Evaluating Other Opinions

To ensure that this type of examination occurs, Opposing Viewpoints books present all types of opinions. Prominent spokespeople on different sides of each issue as well as well-known professionals from many disciplines challenge the reader. An additional goal of the series is to provide a forum for other, less known, or even unpopular viewpoints. The opinion of an ordinary person who has had to make the decision to cut off life support from a terminally ill relative, for example, may be just as valuable and provide just as much insight as a medical ethicist's professional opinion. The editors have two additional purposes in including these less-known views. One, the editors encourage readers to respect others' opinions—even when not enhanced by professional credibility. It is only by reading or listening to and objectively evaluating others' ideas that one can determine whether they are worthy of consideration. Two, the inclusion of such viewpoints encourages the important critical thinking skill of objectively evaluating an author's credentials and bias. This evaluation will illuminate an author's reasons for taking a particular stance on an issue and will aid in readers' evaluation of the author's ideas.

It is our hope that these books will give readers a deeper understanding of the issues debated and an appreciation of the complexity of even seemingly simple issues when good and honest people disagree. This awareness is particularly important in a democratic society such as ours in which people enter into public debate to determine the common good. Those with whom one disagrees should not be regarded as enemies but rather as people whose views deserve careful examination and may shed light on one's own.

Thomas Jefferson once said that "difference of opinion leads to inquiry, and inquiry to truth." Jefferson, a broadly educated man, argued that "if a nation expects to be ignorant and free . . . it expects what never was and never will be." As individuals and as a nation, it is imperative that we consider the opinions of others and examine them with skill and discernment. The Opposing Viewpoints series is intended to help readers achieve this goal.

David L. Bender and Bruno Leone,
Founders

Introduction

"It is not the fault of the gun manufacturer [that] a crime is being committed. We need to put the fault for a crime on the person committing the crime."

Kay Bailey Hutchison,
U.S. senator from Texas

"It's time to send the bill for gun deaths and gun injuries to the gun makers."

Alex Penelas, mayor,
Miami-Dade County, Florida

One day in 1994, Kenzo Dix, a fifteen-year-old boy, was visiting his best friend, Michael, in Berkeley, California. Michael went into his parents' bedroom and returned with a Beretta handgun he had found hidden in his father's nightstand. Michael removed the ammunition clip from the gun, and believing the gun to be unloaded, pointed it at his best friend. Michael later described the scene:

> I look down and I don't even aim. I heard a pop, my eyes opened up and I was shocked. I look and saw Kenzo hunched over, kind of moaning—a creepy moan you don't want to hear. It just stays with you.

Kenzo was shot in the chest and died shortly afterward. His parents sued Beretta, the corporation that manufactured the gun, claiming that the gun was defective because it lacked the safety features that would have prevented the shooting: the Beretta handgun did not indicate that there was a bullet still in the gun's chamber, and Beretta did not design the handgun to prevent an unauthorized user—Michael—from firing it, despite having the technology to do so. The case was not settled until 2004—after three trials. Although the jury eventually found that Beretta was not negligent in Kenzo's death, the Dixes considered their lawsuit a success. California had passed a law in the intervening years requiring many handguns to have safety features such as loaded chamber indicators and locks, features which they believe would have saved their son's life.

In late 1998 the mayors of several American cities sued gun manufacturers and dealers in an attempt to recover their costs associated with gun violence. Their actions resembled the lawsuits filed by many states against the tobacco industry that tried—and in some cases succeeded—to recoup the medical costs associated with smoking. Mayor Marc Morial, on behalf of the city of New Orleans, sued fifteen gun manufacturers and several gun dealers and pawn shops, seeking "reimbursement for millions of dollars" that the city spent to investigate gun crimes and for the medical care of gunshot victims. Dennis Henigan, director of the Legal Action Project of the Center to Prevent Handgun Violence, which served as co-counsel in the case, said the city was suing to "force the gun industry to make a safer, childproof, 'personalized' product." Furthermore, "It's time for the gun industry to be held accountable for the cost of the thousands of tragedies and millions of dollars gun violence inflicts on our nation's cities."

It was not long before the city of Chicago joined in, claiming the gun industry "has created a public nuisance by flooding the streets with weapons deliberately marketed to criminals." While Chicago has tough gun control laws, its neighboring suburbs do not. Mayor Richard M. Daley claimed that gun dealers in these suburbs were catering to gang members by keeping large inventories of guns on hand, knowing that Chicago gang members would buy the weapons and bring them into the city illegally. New York City's lawsuit also alleged that gun manufacturers and dealers were distributing firearms in a manner designed specifically to evade the city's strict gun control laws. Other cities, including Atlanta and Miami, soon followed with lawsuits of their own.

For the gun industry and gun rights supporters, the lawsuits are patently unfair, have no legal merit, and are a roundabout method of imposing gun control. They note that guns are legal to buy, sell, own, and use, and they are perfectly safe if they are used properly. Furthermore, many Americans agree that gun manufacturers should not be held responsible if criminals use guns to shoot people. "You don't sue General Motors when someone drives drunk and hurts someone," argues Anne Kimball, a lawyer for the gun manufacturer Smith & Wesson. Moreover, gun rights activists point out, the gun industry does not have the resources or deep pockets that the tobacco companies have; a successful lawsuit could bankrupt gun manufacturers. Richard Feldman, executive director of the American Shooting Sports Council, warned that the lawsuits filed by New Orleans and other cities "could very well spell an end to the commercial firearm industry in America. Although the public, the facts, and the law are on our side, these alone cannot guarantee that we will prevail." A bankrupt industry would pose enormous difficulties for Americans; hunters, sport shooters, and the American military buy all their weapons from private gun makers.

To ensure that gun manufacturers are not forced to go out of business because of these lawsuits, Congress passed the Protection of Lawful Commerce in Arms Act in 2005. The law proclaims that the gun industry is not "liable for the harm caused by those who criminally or unlawfully misuse firearm products or ammunition products that function as designed and intended." The law further states that making gun manufacturers and dealers responsible for the criminal conduct of others is "an abuse of the legal system [and] erodes public confidence in our Nation's laws." The law nullifies all pending lawsuits against gun manufacturers and prevents other cities from filing new suits. It does not prevent suits against gun manufacturers who produce a defective gun or against dealers who break the law. Thirty states had passed similar legislation that prevented civil lawsuits against gun makers for the criminal misuse of firearms they had produced. The federal law now supersedes all state laws.

The passage of the Protection of Lawful Commerce in Arms Act was applauded by gun rights activists and met with consternation by gun control supporters. The law is just one more illustration of the division that continues to split the country over gun control. In *Opposing Viewpoints: Gun Control*, the authors debate whether gun control is necessary and effective in the following chapters: Is Gun Ownership a Threat to Society? Does the Second Amendment Protect Private Gun Ownership? Do Gun Control Regulations Reduce Crime and Violence? What Measures Would Reduce Gun Violence? This anthology examines the issues when claims of public safety clash with attempts to protect individual rights.

CHAPTER 1

Is Gun Ownership a Threat to Society?

Chapter Preface

The beginning of the 2006–2007 school year was a violent period in schools in North America. In August, Christopher Williams shot and killed his ex-girlfriend's mother, then went to the school in Essex, Vermont, where his ex-girlfriend worked, and shot two teachers, killing one. In mid-September at Dawson College in Montreal, Canada, Kimveer Gill shot twenty students and faculty, killing one student, before turning the gun on himself. Two weeks later in Bailey, Colorado, Duane Morrison sexually assaulted six female students at Platte Canyon High School before shooting and killing one. Three days later, Eric Hainstock, a fifteen-year-old student at Weston Schools in Cazenovia, Wisconsin, shot and killed his principal a day after the principal gave him a disciplinary warning for possession of tobacco. Finally, in early October, Charles Carl Roberts IV entered an Amish schoolhouse in Nickel Mines, Pennsylvania, sent out all the boys and teachers, tied up the ten girl students, then lined them up against the blackboard and shot them, killing five. When the police arrived, he shot himself.

After the shootings, U.S. president George W. Bush told a classroom of students in California, "Our schoolchildren should never fear their safety when they enter into a classroom." The White House, together with the Department of Education and the Department of Justice, organized a conference to determine what could be done to prevent school violence. The Conference on School Safety brought together the president; his attorney general, Alberto Gonzalez; teachers and school administrators; the secretary of the Department of Education; a Florida sheriff; a crisis counselor from Los Angeles; and a survivor of the 1999 Columbine, Colorado, high school shooting, among others. Addressing the conference, Bush told the attendees that classrooms should be "gentle places for learning."

The panel recommended that schools coordinate evacuation and lockdown plans with police; that they should offer more classes in developing good character, mentoring programs, counseling for suicidal teens (who may turn homicidal); and that they should try to get parents more involved in their children's education. The panel discouraged schools from adding metal detectors and additional security cameras because these items often create an atmosphere of being "locked down" and make the students feel that the school is more like a prison. Some panelists advocated stronger gun control laws to keep guns out of the hands of children, which might reduce the number of school shootings.

Despite the wave of school shootings, one expert at the conference maintained that schools remain an extremely safe place for children. Delbert S. Elliott, director of the Center for the Study and Prevention of Violence at the University of Colorado, told the panel that while violence against children—such as fights and attacks by gangs—are increasing, statistics show that teenagers are more likely to be attacked or killed at a shopping mall or at home than on school grounds. "Our kids are safer at school than they are at almost any [other] place," Elliott told the panelists. Of the proposal to add more gun control laws, Gonzales conceded that "obviously, kids should not have access to weapons," but he advocated enforcing current gun control laws rather than enacting new ones.

High-profile cases like the Amish schoolhouse murders focus attention on the issue of gun violence in the nation's schools. The authors in the following chapter debate other issues concerned with whether guns pose a threat to society.

| *"Guns account for 10 percent of all deaths among children ages 5 to 14."*

Guns in the Home Threaten Children's Safety

Jane E. Brody

Jane E. Brody is a syndicated columnist who focuses on health issues. In the following viewpoint, she maintains that guns present a significant safety hazard for children. Children love to explore "secret" hiding spots, Brody argues, where parents often conceal their guns, thinking they are safely hidden; however, Brody reports, unbeknownst to most parents, their children know where guns are hidden in the home—and have handled those guns. In order to protect children from guns, Brody advocates keeping guns unloaded and locked up in a gun safe or strongbox and the key kept in a place where children cannot get to it.

As you read, consider the following questions:

1. According to the author, for each child that is killed by a gunshot wound, how many children are permanently disabled due to injuries from firearms?

2. Of children who have handled firearms in their home, what percentage have done so without their parents' knowledge, as cited by Brody?

3. What is the best solution for keeping children safe from guns, in the author's opinion?

A lthough I wrote about children and gun safety just two years ago [in 2004], the continuing tragedies involving guns in private homes compel me to repeat my plea that all guns be stored safely in a way that keeps children away from them.

In May [2006], the 10-year-old son of a New York City police officer died after accidentally shooting himself in the head with his father's .38-caliber pistol, which he found at home in a closet while looking for a ball.

In June [2006], a 12-year-old New Jersey boy was accidentally killed by his fifth-grade friend while the two were playing with his father's gun, which the children found in an unlocked box.

These are just two of several hundred such deaths that will almost certainly occur this year. Guns account for 10 percent of all deaths among children ages 5 to 14.

For every child who dies from a gunshot wound, three others are injured, and a quarter of those injuries bring on permanent disabilities.

A Familiar Role for Firearms

Most young children are all too familiar with guns, having seen them on television, in the movies or in video games. As a result, some children may not realize that when a real person is shot, he may never get up again.

The most frequent perpetrator in childhood gunshot fatalities and injuries is another child, who may have assumed the gun wasn't loaded or wasn't real. Many children (as well as a good number of adults) can't tell the difference between a real gun and a fake one.

The most frequent sites of childhood encounters with guns are their own homes or the homes of friends or relatives. Children, naturally curious, love to poke around in "secret" places, places where their parents may have hidden a gun, thinking a child would never find it there.

A review of firearm ownership and storage practices in American households, published [in 2004] in *The American Journal of Preventive Medicine*, revealed that "firearms are as likely to be present in U.S. homes with children as in homes without children, and they are often stored in unlocked locations and/or loaded."

This finding prompted two public health specialists, Dr. Frances Baxley of San Francisco General Hospital and Dr. Matthew Miller of the Harvard School of Public Health, to examine what parents know about their children's access to guns in the home.

In the May [2006] issue of *The Archives of Pediatrics and Adolescent Medicine*, the researchers reported that children knew a lot more about the location of guns in the home and were far more likely to have handled those guns than their parents thought. They studied 314 parent-child pairs who lived in homes that had guns, interviewing the parents separately from their children.

Overall, they found that "39 percent of parents who reported that their children were unaware of the storage location of the guns were contradicted by their children's reports." And of the children who said they had handled firearms in the home, only 60 percent were described by their parent as having done so.

Even in homes where all the guns were locked away, the children were as likely to report having handled a gun in the home as were children in homes where guns were stored unlocked.

Homicide, Suicide, and Gun Deaths among Five- to Fourteen-Year-Olds, United States versus Twenty-five Other Nations			
	Gun Homicide	**Nongun Homicide**	**Total**
Homicide			
U.S.	1.22	0.53	1.75
Non-U.S.	0.07	0.23	0.30
Ratio	17:1	2:1	6:1
	Gun Suicide	**Nongun Suicide**	**Total**
Suicide			
U.S.	0.49	0.35	0.84
Non-U.S.	0.05	0.35	0.40
Ratio	10:1	1:1	2:1
Unintentional Gun Death			
U.S.	0.46		
Non-U.S.	0.05		
Ratio	9:0		

Note: The twenty-five other nations are the richest countries with a population greater than one million. Rates are per one hundred thousand (early 1990s).

TAKEN FROM: Data from CDC, 1997b.

Clearly, parents are far too often unaware of how much their children know about the location of guns and what they do with guns kept locked or unlocked in their homes.

"This finding," the authors wrote, "suggests that common preventive measures for ensuring children's safety around household guns often fail to prevent children from gaining unacknowledged access to household guns and may, in fact, lead parents to have misplaced confidence in their ability to accurately predict their children's broader experience with guns in the home."

A further complication is the frequent failure of parents to assure that guns in the homes their children visit are inaccessible to children.

A study led by Dr. Tamera Coyne-Beasley of the University of North Carolina found that one-third of gun owners in the United States with children under age 6 kept a firearm unlocked at home, and guns were kept unlocked in 56 percent of homes where children visited.

The Second-Best Solution

If it were up to me, there would be no guns in any household with children under 18. Better yet, no guns in any household—children or no children. But with half of American homes now in possession of at least one gun, I know this is unlikely to happen. So the second-best measure is to make sure that guns are kept in a place and in a way that children can't get to them.

These are the basic rules of gun safety:

Store all guns unloaded.

Keep your guns locked in a gun safe or a strongbox and carry the key with you or keep it where a child can't get it.

Store all guns separate from their ammunition and keep the ammunition locked as well.

Store your guns out of the sight and the reach of children.

Any gun that cannot be locked away should be stored unloaded with a trigger lock in place at all times.

Make sure you are trained in the proper care, handling and use of any weapon you own.

Check with relatives and the parents of friends your child visits to be sure they practice these gun safety rules.

If your children are old enough and have your permission to handle a gun, make sure they receive safety training from a qualified instructor and use the gun only under adult supervision.

The events surrounding the headline "Boy, 6, Kills Mom During Target Practice" from March 2001 should never have occurred.

The family went target shooting, and the boy was allowed to handle his father's gun. The father stepped away for a moment, and when his son tried to reload the gun, he accidentally shot his mother in the head.

Even if you have no guns at home and would never dream of using one, your children should be taught about guns. First, they must understand that guns are not toys, that violence on television or in the movies is not real, and that guns in real life can cause injury or death.

Second, they must be told never to touch a gun or bullets and to assume that any gun is loaded and can be fired. If they find a gun anywhere or encounter someone handling a gun, they must leave the area at once, go to a safe place and tell an adult what they saw as soon as possible.

> *"The number of toddlers who die from gun accidents is far less than the five hundred children who die in swimming pools each year."*

The Threat of Guns in the Home Is Exaggerated

Wayne LaPierre

Wayne LaPierre, the chief executive officer of the National Rifle Association (NRA), argues in the following viewpoint that the Eddie Eagle GunSafe® program taught by the NRA has been very effective in lowering the accidental death rate from firearms for children. He asserts that more children die from other causes, such as drownings, fires, and accidental poisonings, than from firearms. In addition, LaPierre argues, the gun-ban lobby twists statistics to convince people that more children are killed or injured by guns than really are. In reality, according to LaPierre, the majority of "children" killed by guns are older teens who are engaging in criminal behavior.

As you read, consider the following questions:

1. As cited by LaPierre, what is the simple safety lesson taught by the NRA's Eddie Eagle GunSafe® program?

Wayne LaPierre, "Kids and Guns: Teaching and Tolerance," *Guns, Freedom and Terrorism*, Nashville, TN: Nelson Current, 2003, pp. 172–175. Copyright © 2003 by Wayne LaPierre. All rights reserved. Reproduced by permission.

2. How many children under the age of fourteen are killed every day by guns, according to the author?

3. Who is most likely to be killed by a teenager with a gun, in LaPierre's view?

The National Rifle Association works unceasingly to teach firearms safety and responsibility to America's young people. Safety training—whether it consists of teaching kids how to swim, how to ride a bike, how to avoid strangers, or how to be safe around firearms—is about preventing accidents and saving lives. And that's what the NRA's Eddie Eagle Gun-Safe® Program is all about: preventing accidents and saving young lives.

The Eddie Eagle Program

Offered free of charge, the Eddie Eagle GunSafe® Program helps schools and law enforcement teach gun safety to children in grades K-6. . . . Eddie Eagle uses teacher-tested materials, including an animated video, CDs, cartoon workbooks, and fun safety activities. The hero, Eddie Eagle, teaches a simple safety lesson: "If you see a gun: STOP! Don't Touch. Leave the Area. Tell an Adult." It has been endorsed by the National Sheriffs Association, the Police Athletic League, and state legislatures all over the country. And it won the 1993 Outstanding Community Service Award from the National Safety Council.

Accidental Death Rate Is Declining

Since its introduction in 1988, the Eddie Eagle program has reached more than sixteen million children, thanks to more than twenty thousand instructors, including schoolteachers, police officers, and other community leaders. From its inception to today, the accidental death from firearms rate for children has declined 56 percent, reaching the lowest levels ever recorded in American history, according to the National Center for Health Statistics. . . .

Yet the anti-gun Violence Policy Center (VPC) ran a propaganda campaign against the Eddie Eagle program to smear it, claiming it's just a ploy to sell guns. Never mind that Eddie Eagle never encourages anyone to buy or use a gun. Following the logic of the VPC, then the public should also believe that Smokey [the] Bear markets matches to children, McGruff the Crime Dog markets muggings and drug dealing, and traffic safety programs market cars to kids.

To the gun-ban lobby, Eddie Eagle became a major threat in its drive to indoctrinate America's young people into believing guns are "bad" and "evil"—and they are determined to shut this program down at all costs. Thankfully, their smear campaign failed miserably.

Firearms accidents for all ages, including children, are now at an all-time low. What's the latest data on the number of fatal firearms accidents involving children ages zero to fourteen? For 1999, the latest year for which complete data is available, there were eighty-eight, the lowest number ever recorded. And while any child's death is unspeakably tragic, the fact is that the number of toddlers who die from gun accidents is far less than the five hundred children who die in swimming pools each year. . . .

Twisted Statistics

The latest data available from the Centers for Disease Control (CDC) show that the real number of "children"—people age fourteen or younger—who die from firearms misuse every day is just one. But "one" is a pretty far distance from the numbers cooked up by the gun-prohibition groups. The figures are inflated by claiming that legal adults—those eighteen and nineteen years old—are children.

When you hear statistics about "X children a day killed by guns," you should know that the overwhelming majority of those "children" are older male teenagers. According to the

Gun Safety Education for Youngsters Reduces Accident Rates

A child's death from any cause is a tragedy. In 2000, 600 children and adolescents died of accidental gunshot wounds, 2700 perished in motor vehicle accidents, 3600 children died from burns, 3900 died of drowning, and 12,100 died from poisoning. These are all tragedies, but do we want to ban automobiles, matches, swimming pools, and household chemicals? Firearm accident rates in the United States have been declining steadily since the turn of the century, because of the emphasis placed on gun safety and education courses, including the National Rifle Association's Eddie Eagle program, which has touched in excess of 11 million youngsters in the U.S.

Miguel A. Faria Jr., Medical Sentinel, *vol. 7, no. 4, 2002.*

Centers for Disease Control, there were 3,385 firearms deaths in 1999 of persons under age twenty—or 9.3 a day. Eighty-nine percent were homicides; most of the rest were suicides. The killings are very heavily concentrated geographically in urban inner cities, almost all of which have very repressive gun laws.

Those Most Likely to Be Killed

The persons most likely to be killed by a teenager with a gun are gang members, gang hangers-on, and other teenage criminals. In many killings of inner-city high-school-age persons, the victim is a person who engaged in risky behaviors, such as selling drugs.

A study of teenage gunshot victims in New York City found that 40 percent were shot during hours when they legally should have been in school. Of the children and adolescents injured in drive-by shootings in Los Angeles, "seventy-one percent were gang members." An in-depth study of juvenile delinquents in Philadelphia found that juvenile victims of violent crimes were often perpetrators of such crimes as well. Nationally, a gang member's risk of getting killed is sixty times greater than the general population's risk. A St. Louis study found that the city's youth gang homicide rate unbelievably was one thousand times that of the U.S. general population.

A study of Minneapolis youths arrested for homicide found that 75 percent had been arrested at least once in Minneapolis (the mean number of arrests for this group was 7.8); similarly, 77 percent of Boston youthful homicide perpetrators had a prior Massachusetts court appearance (this group had a mean of 9.7 arraignments). Fifty-nine percent of homicides perpetrated by youths are perpetrated by males while committing another crime, such as robbery or rape.

The solution for nineteen-year-olds who commit murder? It is the same as the solution for twenty-five-year-olds who commit violent felonies: stop the criminal justice revolving door. And stop the revolving door that lets violent predators get away with armed robbery and other violent felonies. If gangsters caught robbing liquor stores couldn't plea-bargain their way out of serious prison time, they wouldn't be on the streets where they could commit a murder.

> *"Assault weapons have been used to perpetrate some of the worst mass murders ever committed in the United States."*

Assault Weapons Are a Threat to Public Safety

Brady Campaign to Prevent Gun Violence

The Brady Campaign to Prevent Gun Violence (BCPGV) is the nation's largest organization dedicated to enacting and enforcing gun control laws. In the following viewpoint, the organization contends that assault weapons—guns that are designed to shoot many bullets very rapidly—are not suitable for hunting, but rather are made specifically for killing people. In fact, BCPGV maintains that some of the worst mass murders in American history were committed with assault weapons. For that reason, the organization supports efforts by law enforcement to ban such weapons.

As you read, consider the following questions:

1. What are the characteristics of an assault weapon, according to the author?

Brady Campaign to Prevent Gun Violence, "Assault Weapons Threaten Public Safety," 2004. www.bradycampaign.org/facts/issues/?page=aw_renew. All information © 2006 Brady Campaign to Prevent Gun Violence. Reproduced by permission.

2. How many rounds of bullets did Patrick Purdy shoot during his two-minute mass murder spree in Stockton, California, according to the BCPGV?

3. According to Jim Pasco, as cited by the author, why are assault weapons not suitable for police use?

The federal law banning the sale of semiautomatic assault weapons, known as the federal assault weapons ban, has expired. It was passed as part of the Violent Crime Control and Law Enforcement Act of 1994. President [Bill] Clinton signed it into law on September 13, 1994. Despite his promise to renew the ban, President George W. Bush and Congress allowed the ban to "sunset" in September of 2004. . . .

Assault Weapons: "Mass-Produced Mayhem"

The guns covered by the Assault Weapons Act were semiautomatic versions of fully automatic guns designed for military use. Whereas an automatic weapon (machine gun) will continue to fire as long as the trigger is depressed (or until the ammunition magazine is emptied), a semiautomatic weapon will fire one round and instantly load the next round with each pull of the trigger. Even semiautomatic assault weapons fire with extraordinary speed. When San Jose, California, police test-fired an UZI, a 30-round magazine was emptied in slightly less than two seconds on full automatic, while the same magazine was emptied in just five seconds on semiautomatic.

The military features of semiautomatic assault weapons are designed to enhance their capacity to shoot multiple targets very rapidly. For example, assault weapons are equipped with large-capacity ammunition magazines that allow the shooter to fire 20, 50, or even more than 100 rounds without having to reload. Pistol grips on assault rifles and shotguns help stabilize the weapon during rapid fire and allow the shooter to spray-fire from the hip position. Barrel shrouds on

Macho Appeal

Assault weapons, while amounting to only 1 percent of America's 190 million privately owned guns, account for a hugely disproportionate share of gun violence precisely because of their macho appeal.

Assault weapons aren't necessary for any kind of hunting or target shooting, but they're popular because they can transform a suburban Walter Mitty into Rambo, for a lot less money than a Hummer.

Nicholas Kristof, New York Times, *August 18, 2004.*

assault pistols protect the shooter's hands from the heat generated by firing many rounds in rapid succession. Far from being simply "cosmetic," these features all contribute to the unique function of any assault weapon to deliver extraordinary firepower. They are uniquely military features, with no sporting purpose whatever.

As ATF [the Bureau of Alcohol, Tobacco, Firearms, and Explosives] has explained:

> Assault weapons were designed for rapid-fire, close-quarter shooting at human beings. That is why they were put together the way they were. You will not find these guns in a duck blind or at the Olympics. *They are mass produced mayhem.*

These weapons "are not generally recognized as particularly suitable for or readily adaptable to sporting purposes" and instead "are attractive to certain criminals." The firepower of assault weapons makes them especially desired by violent criminals and especially lethal in their hands. Prior to the Act, although assault weapons constituted less than 1% of the guns in circulation, they were a far higher percentage of the guns used in crime. ATF's analysis of guns traced to crime showed that assault weapons "are preferred by criminals over law abiding citizens eight to one. . . . Access to them shifts the balance of power to the lawless."

Mass Slayings of Civilians

Assault weapons have been used to perpetrate some of the worst mass murders ever committed in the United States.

- **The McDonald's shooting**—On July 18, 1984, James Huberty killed 21 people and wounded 19 others in a San Ysidro, California, McDonald's using an UZI assault pistol and a shotgun.

- **The Stockton schoolyard massacre**—On January 17, 1989, Patrick Purdy killed 5 small children and wounded 29 others and a teacher at the Cleveland Elementary School in Stockton, California, using a semiautomatic version of the AK-47 assault rifle imported from China. That weapon had been purchased from a gun dealer in Oregon and was equipped with a 75-round "drum" magazine. Purdy shot 106 rounds in less than 2 minutes.

- **The Louisville, Kentucky, workplace massacre**—On September 14, 1989, Joseph Wesbecker killed 7 people and wounded 13 others at his former place of work in Louisville, Kentucky, before taking his own life. Mr. Wesbecker was armed with an AK-47 rifle, two MAC-11 assault pistols, and a duffle-bag full of ammunition.

- **The CIA headquarters shootings**—On January 25, 1993, Pakistani national Mir Aimal Kasi killed 2 CIA employees and wounded 3 others outside the entrance to CIA headquarters in Langley, Virginia. Kasi used a Chinese-made semiautomatic AK-47 assault rifle equipped with a 30-round magazine purchased from a Northern Virginia gun store.

- **The Branch-Davidian standoff in Waco, Texas**—On February 28, 1993, while attempting to serve federal search and arrest warrants at the Branch-Davidian compound in Waco, Texas, four ATF special agents were killed and 16 others were wounded with an arsenal of assault weapons. According to a federal affidavit, the cult had accumulated at least the following assault weapons: 123 AR-15s, 44 AK-47s, 2 Barrett .50 calibers, 2 Street Sweepers, an unknown number of MAC-10 and MAC-11s, 20 100-round drum magazines, and 260 large-capacity banana clips. The weapons were bought legally from gun dealers and at gun shows.

- **The San Francisco Pettit & Martin shootings**—On July 1, 1993, Gian Luigi Ferri killed 8 people and wounded 6 others at the San Francisco law offices of Pettit & Martin and other offices at 101 California Street. Ferri used two TEC-DC9 assault pistols with 50-round magazines. These weapons had been purchased from a pawnshop and a gun show in Nevada.

Threats to Law Enforcement

In the 1980s, law enforcement reported that assault weapons were the "weapons of choice" for drug traffickers, gangs, terrorists, and paramilitary extremist groups. Limiting civilian access to such weapons lessens the need for law enforcement to carry assault weapons themselves in order to match the firepower capability that criminals with assault weapons would have. Law enforcement officers do not want to have to carry M-16s (the military's standard battlefield firearm) as their standard service weapon. In 1997, after a North Hollywood, California, shootout in which police were outgunned by two men with assault weapons, Jim Pasco, executive director of the Fraternal Order of Police stated:

An AK-47 fires a military round. In a conventional home with dry-wall walls, I wouldn't be surprised if it went through six of them. . . . Police are armed with weapons that are effective with criminals in line of sight. They don't want and don't need weapons that would harm innocent bystanders.

For these reasons, law enforcement has been united in support of banning these weapons. . . .

The Federal Assault Weapons Act Was Effective

Firearms deaths increased throughout the 1980s and peaked in 1993 at 39,595. In 1994, the Brady Law and the Assault Weapons Act went into effect. Since then, annual firearm deaths have decreased to 29,573 in 2001, a drop of 25% from the 1994 level. Although there were undoubtedly some other factors that influenced this trend, common sense would suggest that stronger gun laws, including the Assault Weapons Act, played an important role.

> "*Crime rates have not improved as a result of the 1994 [federal assault weapons ban], nor could they be expected to, given the infrequency in which these firearms are used in crime.*"

Assault Weapons Are Not a Threat to Public Safety

Michael Caswell

In the following viewpoint Michael Caswell argues that banning so-called assault weapons will not lower crime rates. Such weapons are used in so few crimes to begin with, he asserts, that taking the firearms out of circulation will make little difference. Furthermore, he maintains, if criminals no longer have easy access to an assault weapon, they will simply use another weapon in its place. Caswell is the executive director of the Web site AWBanSunset.com, an online resource for gun-rights activists against the renewal of the assault weapons ban.

As you read, consider the following questions:

1. According to Caswell, why are assault weapons more likely to be submitted for tracing than other firearms used in crimes?

Michael Caswell, "The Effects of the Ban on Crime," 2004. www.awbansunset.com/effects.html. Reproduced by permission.

2. In the author's opinion, why would it be expected that a ban on assault weapons would result in fewer such firearms being used in crimes?

3. According to the N.I.J. report cited by the author, what were some of the factors that made it difficult to determine the effects of the ban on assault weapons?

The agencies responsible for reporting crime and recordable statistics associated with crime agree. Crime rates *have not improved* as a result of the 1994 [federal assault weapons] ban, *nor could they be expected to*, given the *infrequency* in which these firearms are used in crime. Supporters of the ban present statistics that they claim show the ban "works." From bradycampaign.org:

> In 1999, the National Institute of Justice reported that trace requests for assault weapons declined 20% in the first calendar year after the ban took effect, dropping from 4,077 in 1994 to 3,268 in 1995. Over the same time period, gun murders declined only 10% and trace requests for all types of guns declined 11 percent, clearly showing a greater decrease in the number of assault weapons traced in crime.

It should be noted that, even though the above paragraph stealthily attempts to imply that the ban reduced crime, if you read it carefully, you see that this is not the case (more on this below). Brady Campaign also fails to mention the wealth of other very significant information present in this same report that all but *invalidates their assertion*. For example, with regards to the accuracy of using BATF [Bureau of Alcohol, Tobacco, Firearms, and Explosives], the report states:

> These data are limited because police agencies do not submit a trace request on every gun they confiscate. Many agencies submit very few requests to BATF, particularly in States that maintain gun sales databases (such as California). Therefore, *tracing data are a biased sample* of guns recovered

by police. Prior studies suggest that *assault weapons are more likely to be submitted for tracing* than are other confiscated firearms [emphasis added].

In other words, law enforcement agencies submit trace requests on only a small percentage of firearms used in crime, and the unique appearance of "assault weapons" makes them much more likely to be submitted for a BATF trace compared to, say, a common revolver. So, according to this report, BATF trace data is not valid for this type of study. But, because it is the only available national statistic on types of guns used in crime, the researchers had little choice but to use it (with the disclaimer quote above, conveniently omitted by gun control advocates).

A Critical Point

Furthermore, consider the following:

> ...it appears that, at least in the short term, the grandfathered assault weapons remained largely in dealers' and collectors' inventories instead of leaking into the secondary markets through which criminals tend to obtain guns. ... Offenders could replace the banned guns with legal substitutes or other unbanned semiautomatic weapons to commit their crimes.

This is a critical point that completely offsets Brady's assertion that the ban has had any effect on gun-related crime. Grandfathered firearms (known as "pre-bans") cost significantly more than their "post-ban" near-equivalents; in some cases, new-in-box or mint condition pre-ban AR-15 style rifles can sell for more than double the retail price of post-bans (which aren't exactly cheap either). Disregarding the inaccuracy of trace requests as a reliable statistic, common sense says a decrease in the use of these particular firearms in crime is exactly what would be expected. Why would a criminal go through the hassle and expense of trying to obtain a banned

The Use of Assault Weapons in Crime

Looking at the broader picture of all gun use in crime, it becomes clear that *"assault weapons" are a minor part of the problem.* Police gun seizure data from around the nation finds that "assault weapons" account for less than 2% of guns seized by the police; more typically, they account for *less than 1%,* according to data compiled from 24 major jurisdictions.

At first blush one might say that the lack of crime using assault weapons or high-capacity magazines is due to the ban. Wrong. Before the ban the AK and AR type rifles, two of the most common, were produced in the millions.

Steve Martin, "The Use of 'Assault Weapons' in Crime,"
www.awbansunset.com/crime.html.

"assault weapon" if there were plenty of other guns that would do the job just as well and were freely available? And, of course, on top of all this, "assault weapons" were *very rarely used in crime even before the ban.*

An Analogy to Prove the Point

Here is an analogy to help illustrate this point. Suppose an organization decides it does not like people driving, for example, Honda Civics that have all sorts of radical body modifications and attachments (spoilers, hood scoops, etc.), giving these cars a sporty, racy look. While these features are primarily cosmetic in nature, some people just don't like the way these cars look, convinced that only the most reckless and irresponsible drivers own them, and manage to get the local government to ban the manufacture of any new automobile with a race car-like appearance. For the people who like these cars, the ban has the effect of turning them into collector's items virtually overnight, and prices skyrocket. Because of this, and because no new ones are being produced, there are not nearly as many of them available to the average person. . . . Most are securely locked away in collectors' garages.

After a few years, the group that called for the ban gathers statistics on speeding tickets and accidents, which naturally reflect the effects of the ban, showing a reduced number of traffic citations issued to drivers of these cars, though not an overall reduction in citations. The group claims victory, citing the reduction in traffic violations for this particular style of car, but ignores the fact that the small number of bad drivers who previously drove the cosmetically incorrect cars now simply drive other cars (and do so just as recklessly). The overall violation rate remains the same as it would have without the ban. *But by selectively taking a very small part of the statistics out of context, the organization attempts to manipulate the masses into believing the legislation had a positive effect on public safety,* when it has actually had virtually no detectable effect at all.

Assault Weapons Are Rarely Used

The N.I.J. report cited by Brady also makes quite a few other significant points, such as:

> A number of factors—including the fact that the banned weapons and magazines were *rarely used to commit murders* in this country. . .posed challenges in discerning the effects of the ban [emphasis added].

> . . .about half the banned makes and models were rifles, which are hard to conceal for criminal use.

> . . .the banned guns are used in only a *small fraction of gun crimes*; even before the ban, most of them rarely turned up in law enforcement agencies' requests to the Bureau of Alcohol, Tobacco and Firearms (BATF) to trace the sales histories of guns recovered in criminal investigations [emphasis added].

...other analyses using a variety of national and local data sources found *no clear ban effects* on certain types of murders that were thought to be more closely associated with the rapid-fire features of assault weapons and other semiautomatics equipped with large capacity magazines. *The ban did not produce declines* in the average number of victims per incident of gun murder or gun murder victims with multiple wounds [emphasis added].

There were several reasons to expect, *at best*, a modest ban effect on criminal gun injuries and deaths. First, studies before the ban generally found that between *less than 1 and 8 percent of gun crimes* involved assault weapons, depending on the specific definition and data source used [emphasis added].

Murders of police by offenders armed with assault weapons declined from an estimated 16 percent of gun murders of police in 1994 and early 1995 to 0 percent in the latter half of 1995 and early 1996. However, *such incidents are sufficiently rare* that the available data *do not permit a reliable assessment* of whether this contributed to a general reduction in gun murders of police [emphasis added].

Given the limited use of the banned guns and magazines in gun crimes, even the *maximum theoretically achievable preventive effect* of the ban on outcomes such as the gun murder rate is almost certainly *too small to detect statistically...* [emphasis added].

The public safety benefits of the 1994 ban have not yet been demonstrated.

This report, despite being sponsored by the Federal government during the [Bill] Clinton administration, clearly presents significantly more evidence that proves why the ban should *not* be renewed than it does supporting the ban....

Not Again!

It would seem then that the only folks affected by this silly bit of legislation are the honest, law-abiding citizens who own guns. Given the gun control objective of disarming citizens, we must now draw the line in the sand and state unequivocally, "Not my rights, not again!"

> "Criminals surveyed report being more
> afraid of encountering armed victims
> than they are of encountering the po-
> lice."

Laws That Allow Concealed Weapons Protect Society

Michael Huemer

*In the following viewpoint Michael Huemer notes that a study
that examined the crime rates for every county in the United
States found that the rates in counties where citizens were allowed to carry concealed weapons were half that of counties
where residents could not carry concealed weapons. Huemer thus
argues that when law-abiding citizens are allowed to carry concealed weapons, criminals do not know who has a gun and who
does not and so are less likely to commit a violent crime, because
they might get shot. Huemer is a professor of philosophy at the
University of Colorado.*

As you read, consider the following questions:

1. According to studies cited by the author, how often are
   guns estimated to be used in self-defense each year?

Michael Huemer, "Is There a Right to Own a Gun?" *Social Theory and Practice*, vol.
29, April 2003, pp. 297–324. Copyright © 2003 by *Social Theory and Practice*. Reproduced by permission of the publisher and the author.

2. What requirements are necessary before Gary Kleck and Marc Gertz consider a gun use to be a "defensive gun use," in Huemer's opinion?

3. What are the differences between "discretionary" and "shall-issue" permit laws, according to the author?

Guns are used surprisingly often by private citizens in the United States for self-defense purposes. Fifteen surveys, excluding the one discussed in the following paragraph, have been conducted since 1976, yielding estimates of between 760,000 and 3.6 million defensive gun uses per year, the average estimate being 1.8 million. Probably among the more reliable is [Gary] Kleck and [Marc] Gertz's 1993 national survey, which obtained an estimate of 2.5 million annual defensive gun uses, excluding military and police uses and excluding uses against animals. Gun users in 400,000 of these cases believe that the gun certainly or almost certainly saved a life. While survey respondents almost certainly overestimated their danger, if even one-tenth of them were correct, the number of lives saved by guns each year would exceed the number of gun homicides and suicides. For the purposes of Kleck and Gertz's study, a "defensive gun use" requires respondents to have actually seen a person (as opposed, for example, to merely hearing a suspicious noise in the yard) whom they believed was committing or attempting to commit a crime against them, and to have at a minimum threatened the person with a gun, but not necessarily to have fired the gun. Kleck's statistics imply that defensive gun uses outnumber crimes committed with guns by a ratio of about 3:1. While Kleck's statistics could be an overestimate, one should bear three points in mind before relying on such a hypothesis to discount the defensive value of guns. First, Kleck's figures would have to be very large overestimates in order for the harms of guns to exceed their benefits. Second, one would have to suppose that all fifteen of the surveys alluded to have contained overestimates. Third, it is not clear prima facie that an overestimate is more likely than an underestimate; perhaps some respondents either invent or misdescribe incidents, but perhaps also some respondents either forget or prefer not to discuss their defensive gun uses with a stranger on the telephone.

The National Crime Victimization Survey

One survey, the National Crime Victimization Survey [NCVS], obtained an estimate an order of magnitude below the others. The NCVS statistics imply something in the neighborhood of 100,000 defensive gun uses per year. Though even this number would establish a significant self-defense value of guns, the NCVS numbers are probably a radical underestimate, given their extreme divergence from all other estimates. Kleck describes the methodological flaws of the NCVS, one of the more serious being that the NCVS is a nonanonymous survey (respondents provide their addresses and telephone numbers) which the respondents know to be sponsored by the U.S. Justice Department. Respondents may hesitate to nonanonymously report their defensive gun uses to employees of the law enforcement branch of the federal government, particularly if they believe there is any chance that they might be accused of doing anything illegal. In addition, respondents are not asked specifically about defensive gun uses, but are merely invited in a general way to describe anything they did for self-protection. And respondents are not asked about self-protective actions unless they have previously answered affirmatively to the crime victimization questions, and it is known that the NCVS drastically underestimates at least domestic violence incidents; only 22% of domestic assaults appearing in police records (which may themselves be incomplete) were mentioned by respondents to the survey.

The Benefits of Concealed Weapons

In the United States, some states prohibit the carrying of concealed weapons. Others have "discretionary" permit laws,

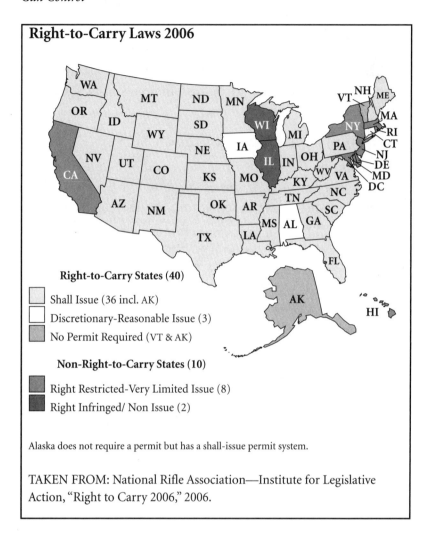

Right-to-Carry Laws 2006

Right-to-Carry States (40)

☐ Shall Issue (36 incl. AK)

☐ Discretionary-Reasonable Issue (3)

▨ No Permit Required (VT & AK)

Non-Right-to-Carry States (10)

▨ Right Restricted-Very Limited Issue (8)

▨ Right Infringed/ Non Issue (2)

Alaska does not require a permit but has a shall-issue permit system.

TAKEN FROM: National Rifle Association—Institute for Legislative Action, "Right to Carry 2006," 2006.

meaning that local officials may, at their discretion, issue permits to carry concealed weapons to citizens who apply for such permits (in such states, officials commonly restrict permits to citizens with special circumstances, such as jobs that require them to carry large sums of money). Others have "nondiscretionary" or "shall-issue" laws, which require officials to issue permits to all applicants who meet specified, objective conditions (these conditions may include absence of a criminal record, payment of a fee, some minimum age, and/or completion of a firearms safety course). Shall-issue laws result in many more permits being issued. Finally, the state of Vermont allows the carrying of concealed weapons with no need for a permit. Several discretionary states converted to nondiscretionary laws during the 1980s and 1990s.

John Lott and David Mustard conducted a study, probably the most rigorous and comprehensive study in the gun control literature, on the effects of nondiscretionary laws on crime rates. Lott's study uses time-series and cross-sectional data for all 3,054 counties in the United States from 1977 to 1992. Overall, states with shall-issue laws have a violent crime rate just over half (55%) of the rate in other states. This alone does not establish that the more restrictive gun laws are a *cause* of the dramatically higher violent crime rates in the states that have them, since the correlation could be explained by the hypothesis that states that already have higher crime rates are more likely to pass restrictive gun laws. The latter hypothesis, however would not explain why violent crime rates fell after states adopted shall-issue concealed carry laws. After performing a multiple-regression analysis to control for numerous other variables—such as arrest and conviction rates, prison sentence lengths, population density, income levels, and racial and gender makeup of counties—Lott found that upon the adoption of shall-issue laws, murder rates declined immediately by about 8%, rapes by 5%, and aggravated assaults by 7%, with declines continuing in subsequent years (Lott explains the latter fact by the gradually increasing numbers of individuals obtaining permits).

More Guns Mean Less Crime

Gun control proponents may find these statistics theoretically surprising: increasing the availability of one important means of committing violent crimes, they believe, should increase the violent crime rate. But an alternative theory gives the opposite prediction: Increased availability of guns to citizens, including the ability to carry concealed weapons, increases the risks to would-be criminals of experiencing undesired consequences as a result of attempting a violent crime. These consequences include being shot, being detained by the would-be victim until the police arrive, and simply being unable to complete the crime. Thus, other things being equal, increased availability of guns to the general public should result in decreased violent crime.

Gun Control Laws Hurt the Innocent, Not Criminals

Lott's study strongly corroborates this theory. But even before considering statistical evidence, the theory is more plausible than that offered by gun control supporters. Gun control laws tend to influence the behavior of would-be crime victims much more than the behavior of criminals. Those who are willing to commit violent felonies are much more likely than the average citizen to be willing to commit misdemeanors such as carrying a concealed weapon without a permit. They are also more likely to have black market contacts capable of supplying them with illegal weapons. Thus, laws that prohibit or place obstacles in the way of carrying concealed weapons, or owning weapons at all, are likely to cause a much greater reduction in the proportion of armed victims than in the proportion of armed criminals. Furthermore, one can guess that the possibility of encountering an armed victim probably has a greater effect on would-be criminals, with respect to deterring violent crimes, than would a moderate increase in the difficulty of obtaining a gun to assist in crimes, since the feared consequences of attacking an armed victim are extremely serious, whereas increased difficulty in obtaining a gun is a relatively small impediment to committing a violent crime, particularly if one can choose a victim who is physically weaker than oneself and unarmed, or if one has black market contacts. This argument is inconclusive, since it could be that very few noncriminals would carry guns for self-protection even if allowed to, in which case the risk to criminals of encountering armed victims would still be a minor factor. But in fact, a great many noncriminal Americans presently own guns, and approximately 9% of Americans surveyed admit to carrying a gun for self-protection outside the home. Accordingly, criminals surveyed report being more afraid of encountering armed victims than they are of encountering the police.

For these reasons, one should not be surprised that the effect of stricter gun laws of reducing a deterrent to violent crime should predominate over their effect of making it harder to obtain tools for assisting in such crimes.

"There is little evidence that the [concealed-carry] laws effectively deter would-be assailants and thieves."

Laws That Allow Concealed Weapons Do Not Make Society Safer

Adam Lichtenheld

In the following viewpoint Adam Lichtenheld argues that allowing people to carry concealed weapons in public is a dangerous idea. He asserts that there is little evidence that concealed-carry laws deter criminals from committing crimes. Lichtenheld also maintains that would-be criminals may also carry concealed weapons and that concealed-carry laws make it easier for criminals to steal guns from law-abiding citizens. Furthermore, he contends, there are very few instances in which a gun has been used in self-defense in public. Lichtenheld was a sophomore at the University of Wisconsin at Madison at the time he wrote this viewpoint in 2005. He has won several journalism awards for his writing.

As you read, consider the following questions:

1. As of October 2005, how many states have do-not-issue concealed-carry permits for their residents, according to Lichtenheld?

2. To what does the author credit the decrease in crime rates across the country?

3. What percentage of law enforcement officers are shot with their own weapon, as cited by Lichtenheld?

Last week [mid-October 2005], two [Wisconsin] state legislators finally introduced the controversial Personal Protection Act, a proposal that would allow citizens to bear a gun, knife or—as ridiculous as it sounds—a billy club in public. The bill's drafters include every gun-lover's hero, Sen. Dave Zien, R-Eau Claire, a man with more rifles and shotguns on his office walls than the Madison police, and Rep. Scott Gunderson, R-Waterford, the Assembly's alleged hunting expert.

Succumbing to the Gun Lobby

Undercutting progressive gun-control initiatives, state politicians around the country have bowed to the [National Rifle Association]-rabid right and their backward "more guns, less crime" rhetoric in their absurd belief that hidden handguns deter crime, that everyone would be afraid to harm anyone else out of fear that a weapon is shoved down every pocket. This has spawned the passage of laws in almost every state to allow citizens to carry concealed firearms in public. Wisconsin, as one of four remaining states that ha[ve] thus far rejected political conformity, is now threatening to succumb to the pressures of the gun lobby.

While alarmists like to predict a chaotic scene reminiscent of the Wild West, there are many risks associated with allowing citizens to sport hidden handguns whose logic is more concrete than fantastic predictions of "Matrix"-style shootouts on [Madison's] Bascom Hill.

Concealed Weapons Are Dangerous

Even the gun lobby agrees that concealed weapons aren't safe. Every time a concealed carry law passes . . . , there's always clauses in there that make sure to keep concealed weapons away from schools, churches, bars, sports stadiums, and government buildings. Why? Because concealed weapons are too dangerous to take to those places.

But what the gun lobby doesn't get, and what most Americans know, is that concealed weapons are dangerous *anywhere*. There's no reason to single out schools and churches—if concealed weapons don't belong there, they don't belong anywhere on the streets.

Gun Guys, "Most Americans Are Against Concealed Weapons,"
March 28, 2006. www.gunguys.com/?p=885.

In support of their legislation, Messrs. Zien and Gunderson have continually quoted a flawed study by gun-loving economist John Lott, whose linking of concealed-carry laws to lower crime rates has been frequently debunked by a multitude of esteemed scholars and pro-gun criminologists. Just as there is minimal proof that conceal and carry brings out the Clint Eastwood in every citizen, there is little evidence that the laws effectively deter would-be assailants and thieves. Rapid decreases in crime rates across the nation can be more directly associated with strict gun access laws and post-Sept. 11 security initiatives than weak provisions that allow individuals to bring their pistol to the supermarket.

A Bad Idea

You don't need to be a staunch anti-gun advocate to see why letting people carry guns in banks, churches, university dormitories, and the state Capitol is a fundamentally bad idea.

While granting citizens the means to protect themselves, it also gives criminals the means to commit crimes. Concealed-carry extends more rights to crooks and felons, guaranteeing that some weapons will fall into the wrong hands, making law-enforcement a virtual nightmare. Perhaps this is why the Wisconsin Chiefs of Police Association strongly opposes the Zien-Gunderson bill.

Police, more than anybody, would know how the presence of a handgun endangers all parties, including the gun's owner—for 12 percent of law enforcement officers killed by firearms are shot to death with their own service weapon. Guns quickly escalate a situation, and bringing one into the fold—imagine a drunken brawl or back alley mugging—only stands to make things much, much worse. You go from losing your wallet to losing your life; you go from enduring a black eye or a bloody nose to suffering from a gunshot wound.

Proponents of the legislation especially love to claim that conceal and carry is necessary for self-defense. Yet the odds that one would use a gun on an assailant or thief are quite minimal—of the over 30,000 gun deaths in 2002, only 163 were deemed "justifiable homicide," and it's well known that a gun is 43 times more likely to be used in killing its owner or a relative than an intruder. The legislation, which is opposed by a majority of Wisconsin citizens and state gun owners, is supposedly intended to protect the disabled and the elderly. Yet these are the very people who would have the most difficult time obtaining the necessary gun permit, and the citizens who would be most incapable of effectively operating a firearm at all.

Not the Solution

In America, guns are presented as the solution to everything. Too many school shootings? Give teachers firearms. Airplane hijackings becoming a problem? Arm the pilots. Too many criminals running loose? Let citizens wield their semiautomatics and use the law at their own discretion. In a nation where gun violence remains a virtual epidemic, the very poison itself is also assumed to be the [antidote]. If more guns lead to less crime, then why does the United States, with the developing world's most lax gun laws, suffer from 93 gun deaths every day, four to five times more than any other industrialized nation? If owning a weapon makes people safer, then why does a gun in the home triple the risk of homicide? If gun accessibility is not a problem, then why do firearm fatalities remain as the second leading killer of this nation's youth? Other states have bowed to our fear-driven culture and the junk science it produces, undermining rapid advancements in curtailing crime and dealing a blow to effective gun control. I would hate to see Wisconsin do the same.

Periodical Bibliography

The following articles have been selected to supplement the diverse views presented in this chapter.

Eric W. Alexy | "Right-to-Carry Laws Conceal Guns, Facts," *Columbia Chronicle*, September 2003. www.columbiachronicle.com

Jordan Carleo-Evangelist | "Guns and Crime: The Great Debate," *Albany (NY) Times Union*, October 18, 2004. www.timesunion.com.

Christian Science Monitor | "All Gun Control Can't Be Local," May 3, 2006.

Bill Durston | "Terminate This Epidemic," *Sacramento (CA) News & Review*, August 5, 2004. www.newsreview.com/sacramento/Home.

Gene Healy | "Less Guns, More Crime," *American Spectator*, January 20, 2004.

Harvard Hollenberg | "Let's Give the NRA What It Really Wants," *New York Law Journal*, October 12, 2004.

Abigail Kohn et al. | "Straight Shooting on Gun Control: A *Reason* Debate," *Reason*, May 2005.

Dave Kopel | "Bait-n-Switch," *National Review Online*, September 13, 2004. www.nationalreview.com.

John R. Lott Jr. | "The Big Lie of the Assault Weapons Ban," *Los Angeles Times*, June 28, 2005.

John R. Lott Jr. | "Don't Blame Hunters," *New York Post*, February 16, 2006.

John R. Lott Jr. | "A Girl's Guide to Guns," *New York Post*, January 1, 2006.

Howard M. Metzenbaum | "America Wants the Assault Weapons Ban," *Washington Post*, July 19, 2004.

OPPOSING
VIEWPOINTS®
SERIES

CHAPTER 2

Does the Second Amendment Protect Private Gun Ownership?

Chapter Preface

The Second Amendment's unusual phrasing and punctuation—"A well regulated militia being necessary to the security of a free State, the right of the People to keep and bear arms, shall not be infringed"—keeps gun control supporters and opponents at odds with each other as they argue over the amendment's meaning. At issue is whether the Founding Fathers intended the right to keep and bear arms to be a collective right—one that ensures that militias are not disarmed by the government—or whether it is an individual right, meant to guarantee that anyone who wants to own a gun can do so without fear of government interference.

In the debate over the words "the people" in the Second Amendment, gun rights advocates cite a 1990 opinion written by U.S. Supreme Court justice William H. Rehnquist in *United States v. Verdugo-Urquidez*. Rehnquist wrote that "'the people' protected by the Fourth Amendment, and by the First and Second Amendments, and to whom rights and powers are reserved in the Ninth and Tenth Amendments, refers to a class of persons who are part of a national community." Therefore, Don B. Kates Jr., a prominent gun rights proponent, concludes, "If 'the people' really meant the right of states to maintain a militia, then we would be left with the absurd notion that only the states have the right to peaceably assemble, only the states have the right to be secure in their persons and property, etc." Consequently, gun control opponents contend, "the right of the People to keep and bear arms" is an individual right.

Gun control proponents, however, use another Supreme Court case to support their view that the Second Amendment is meant to protect a collective right to own a gun, not an individual right. In *United States v. Miller*, decided in 1939, the Supreme Court found (and lower courts have followed its interpretation in rulings in other cases) that the sawed-off shot-gun at issue in the case had no practical purpose in a militia and therefore it did not enjoy the Second Amendment's protections. What this means, according to gun control supporters, is that the amendment's protections are for the collective (i.e., militias') right to keep and bear arms and that the government has the power and authority to regulate the use and sale of firearms.

Since gun control advocates and opponents both have rulings from the U.S. Supreme Court to support their position on the meaning of the Second Amendment, the debate is sure to continue for some time. The authors in the following chapter debate the meaning of the Second Amendment and whether it permits or prohibits gun control.

> "Second Amendment protections were not intended for the state but for each individual against the state—a deterrent to government tyranny."

The Individual Right to Bear Arms Is Guaranteed by the Second Amendment

Robert A. Levy

In the following viewpoint, Robert A. Levy argues that the Second Amendment guarantees a right to bear arms to the individual, not to the collective. He maintains that the right to bear arms is justified by the phrase "a well-regulated militia" and is secured by the phrase "the right of the people . . . shall not be infringed." Levy supports his argument with references to several court cases in which the justices found that the Constitution protects individual rights, as well as briefs filed by the Justice Department that assert that the right to bear arms is an individual right. Levy is a senior fellow in Constitutional Studies at the Cato Institute.

Robert A. Levy, "Testimony Before the House Committee on Government Reform," June 28, 2005. www.cato.org. Reproduced by permission.

As you read, consider the following questions:

1. In the author's opinion, how would the Second Amendment read if it were meant to protect the rights of a militia?
2. What was the Fifth Circuit Court's ruling in *U.S. v. Emerson*, as cited by Levy?
3. How does the decision by the U.S. Supreme Court in U.S. v. Miller differ from that of *Emerson*, according to the author?

A question that has perplexed legal scholars for decades goes like this: Does the right to keep and bear arms belong to us as individuals, or does it belong to us collectively as members of a militia? The answer has now been documented in an extended and scholarly staff memorandum opinion prepared for the Attorney General and released to the public [in 2004]. The memorandum opinion concluded that "The Second Amendment secures a right of individuals generally, not a right of States or a right restricted to persons serving in militias."

I concur. The main clause of the Second Amendment ("the right of the people to keep and bear Arms, shall not be infringed") secures the right. The subordinate clause ("A well regulated Militia, being necessary to the security of a free State") justifies the right. Properly understood, the militia clause helps explain why we have a right to bear arms. A well-regulated militia is a sufficient but not necessary condition to the exercise of that right. Imagine if the Second Amendment said, "A well-educated Electorate, being necessary to self-governance in a free state, the right of the people to keep and read Books shall not be infringed." Surely, no one would suggest that only registered voters (i.e., members of the electorate) would have a right to read. Yet that is precisely the effect if the Second Amendment is interpreted to apply only to members of a militia.

The Right of the People

If the Second Amendment truly meant what the collective rights advocates propose, then the text would read, "A well regulated Militia being necessary to the security of a free State, the right of the states [or the state militias] to keep and bear arms shall not be infringed." But the Second Amendment, like the First and Fourth Amendments, refers explicitly to "the right of the people." Consider the placement of the amendment within the Bill of Rights, the part of the Constitution that deals exclusively with the rights of individuals. There can be no doubt that First Amendment rights like speech and religion belong to us as individuals. Similarly, Fourth Amendment protections against unreasonable searches are individual rights. In the context of the Second Amendment, we secure "the right of the people" by guaranteeing the right of each person. Second Amendment protections were not intended for the state but for each individual against the state—a deterrent to government tyranny. Here's how Ninth Circuit judge Alex Kozinski put it: "The institution of slavery required a class of people who lacked the means to resist. . . . All too many of the . . . great tragedies of history—Stalin's atrocities, the killing fields of Cambodia, the Holocaust—were perpetrated by armed troops against unarmed populations."

Maybe the threat of tyrannical government is less today than it was when our republic was experiencing its birth pangs. But incompetence by the state in defending its citizens is a greater threat. The demand for police to defend us increases in proportion to our inability to defend ourselves. That's why disarmed societies tend to become police states. Witness law-abiding inner-city residents, disarmed by gun control, begging for police protection against drug gangs— despite the terrible violations of civil liberties that such protection entails (e.g., curfews, anti-loitering laws, civil asset forfeiture, nonconsensual searches of public housing, and even video surveillance of residents in high crime areas). An unarmed citizenry creates the conditions that lead to tyranny. The right to bear arms is thus preventive; it reduces the demand for a police state. When people are incapable of protecting themselves, they become either victims of the criminals or dependents of the state.

What the Courts Have Ruled

What do the courts have to say? In a 2001 Texas case, *United States v. Emerson*, the Fifth Circuit held that the Constitution "protects the right of individuals, including those not then actually a member of any militia . . . to privately possess and bear their own firearms . . . suitable as personal individual weapons." That constitutional right is not absolute, said the court. For example, killers do not have a constitutional right to possess weapons of mass destruction. Some persons and some weapons may be restricted. Indeed, the Fifth Circuit held that Emerson's Second Amendment rights could be temporarily curtailed because there was reason to believe he posed a threat to his estranged wife. And the Tenth Circuit, in *United States v. Haney*, ruled that machine guns were not the type of weapon protected by the Second Amendment. The Supreme Court declined to review either case.

The high court has not decided a Second Amendment case since *United States v. Miller* in 1939. On that occasion, the challenged statute required registration of machine guns, sawed off rifles, sawed off shotguns, and silencers. First, said the Court, "militia" means all males physically capable of acting in concert for the common defense. That suggested a right belonging to all of us, as individuals. But the Court also held that the right extended only to weapons rationally related to a militia—not the sawed off shotgun questioned in *Miller*. That mixed ruling has puzzled legal scholars for more than six decades. If military use is the decisive test, then citizens can possess rocket launchers and missiles. Obviously, that is not what the Court had in mind. Indeed, anti-gun advocates, who regularly cite *Miller* with approval, would be apoplectic if the Court's military-use doctrine were logically extended.

Because *Miller* is so murky, it can only be interpreted narrowly, allowing restrictions on weapons, like machine guns and silencers, with slight value to law-abiding citizens, and high value to criminals. In other words, *Miller* applies to the type of weapon, not to the question whether the Second Amendment protects individuals or members of a militia. That's the conclusion the Fifth Circuit reached in *Emerson*. It found that *Miller* upheld neither the individual rights model of the Second Amendment nor the collective rights model. *Miller* simply decided that the weapons at issue were not protected.

Enter former U.S. Attorney General John Ashcroft. First, in a letter to the National Rifle Association, he reaffirmed a long-held opinion that all law-abiding citizens have an individual right to keep and bear arms. Ashcroft's letter was supported by 18 state attorneys general, including six Democrats, then followed by two Justice Department briefs, filed with the Supreme Court in the *Haney* and *Emerson* cases. For the first time, the federal government argued against the collective rights position in formal court papers.

Permissible Exceptions

Despite Ashcroft's view of the Second Amendment, the Justice Department declared that both *Emerson* and *Haney* were correctly decided. In *Emerson*, the restriction on persons subject to a domestic violence restraining order was a permissible exception to Second Amendment protection. And in *Haney*, the ban on machine guns applied to a type of weapon uniquely susceptible to criminal misuse.

Many legal scholars are now taking that same position. Harvard's Alan Dershowitz, a former ACLU [American Civil Liberties Union] board member, says he "hates" guns and

Not for the National Guard

Article I, Section 10 of the Constitution states,

No State shall, *without the Consent of Congress,* lay any Duty of Tonnage, *keep Troops,* or Ships of War in times of Peace, enter into any Agreement or Compact with another State, or with a foreign Power, or *engage in War,* unless actually invaded, or in such imminent Danger as will not admit of delay.

It would seem that explicit language prohibiting the "keeping of troops," in one of the first sections of the Constitution, is considerably at odds with those who argue that the Bill of Rights (that was added only somewhat later) was guaranteeing that right to the states.

Andy Barniskis, March 28, 2003. www.keepandbeararms.com.

wants the Second Amendment repealed. But he condemns "foolish liberals who are trying to read the Second Amendment out of the Constitution by claiming it's not an individual right. . . . They're courting disaster by encouraging others to use the same means to eliminate portions of the Constitution they don't like." Harvard's Laurence Tribe, another respected liberal scholar, and Yale professor Akhil Amar acknowledge that there is an individual right to keep and bear arms, albeit limited by "reasonable regulation in the interest of public safety." In that respect, Tribe and Amar agree with the *Emerson* court and with Ashcroft on two fundamental issues: First, the Second Amendment confirms an individual rather than a collective right. Second, that right is not absolute; it is subject to regulation. To the extent there is disagreement, it hinges on what constitutes permissible regulation—i.e., where to draw the line.

Underlying Constitutional Points

To reinforce the views of Dershowitz, Tribe, Amar, and Ashcroft, let me comment briefly on a few of the underlying constitutional points.

- Three provisions limit the states' power over the militia. Article I, section 8, grants Congress the power to "organiz[e], arm, and disciplin[e], the militia." Article I, section 10, says that "No state shall, without the consent of Congress, . . . keep troops in time of peace." Article II, section 2, declares the "President shall be Commander in Chief . . . of the Militia of the several States." Given those three provisions, how could the Second Amendment secure a state's right to arm the militia? No one argued then or argues now that the Second Amendment repealed all three earlier provisions.

- Consider the Supreme Court's pronouncement in *Miller*: "When called for service [in an organized militia] these men were expected to appear bearing arms supplied by themselves." If militia members were to arm themselves, the Second Amendment could not refer to states arming militias. Furthermore, if the *Miller* Court thought the Second Amendment merely enabled states to arm their militias, the Court would have dismissed the case on standing grounds. The plaintiff, *Miller*, was not a state and therefore had no standing to sue. The Court would never have reached the question whether a sawed off shotgun had military utility.

- Multiple provisions in the Bill of Rights refer to the right "of the people." In a 1990 case, *United States v. Verdugo-Urquidez*, the Court said, "'the people' protected by the Fourth Amendment, and by the First and Second Amendments, and to whom rights and powers are reserved in the Ninth and Tenth Amendments, refers to a class of persons who are part of a national community or have otherwise developed sufficient connection with this country to be considered part of that community." That statement contains no mention or even suggestion of a collective right

- What about the militia clause? That syntax was not unusual for the times. For example, the free press clause of the 1842 Rhode Island Constitution stated: "The liberty of the press being essential to the security of freedom in a state, any person may publish his sentiments of any subject." That provision surely does not mean that the right to publish protects only the press. It protects "any person"; and one reason among others that it protects any person is that a free press is essential to a free society.

- In the Militia Act of 1792, *militia* is defined as "every free able-bodied white male citizen ... who is or shall be of the age of 18 years, and under the age of 45 years." That definition is expanded in the Modern Militia Act (1956–58) to read "all able-bodied males at least 17 years of age and ... under 45 yrs of age [and] female citizens ... who are members of the National Guard." The Act goes on to state that "the classes of the militia are (1) the organized militia, which consists of the National Guard and the Naval Militia; and (2) the unorganized militia, which consists of [all other members]." Ninth Circuit judge Andrew J. Kleinfeld wrote that the "militia is like the jury pool, consisting of 'the people,' limited, like the jury pool, to those capable of performing the service."

- Next, consider this historical context: Anti-federalists wanted three major changes prior to ratifying the Constitution: (1) include a Bill of Rights, (2) give states, not the federal government, power to arm the militia, and (3) eliminate federal power to maintain a standing army. Here was the federalist response, addressing those demands in reverse order: (1) Don't worry about the federal government maintaining a standing army; the federal militia power will obviate that need. (2) Don't worry about federal control over the militia; armed individuals will obviate those concerns. And (3) to ensure that individuals have a right to be armed, we will include such a provision in a Bill of Rights. So the federalist position depended on the people being armed. Clearly, the addition of the Second Amendment could not have been intended to eliminate that right. The Second Amendment's prefatory clause was the federalists' way of pacifying anti-federalists without limiting the power of the federal government to maintain a standing army or increasing the states' power over the militia.

- Here's a parallel view of that history, interpreting the term "well-regulated." In its 18th century context, well-regulated did not mean heavily regulated, but rather, properly, not overly regulated. Looked at in that manner, the Second Amendment ensured that militias would not be improperly regulated—even weakened—by disarming the citizens who would be their members. The Framers feared and distrusted standing armies; so they provided for a militia (all able-bodied males above the age of 17) as a counterweight. But the Framers also realized, in granting Congress near-plenary power over the militia, that a select, armed subset—like today's National Guard—could be equivalent to a standing army. So they wisely crafted the Second Amendment to forbid Congress from disarming other citizens, thereby ensuring a "well-regulated" militia.

For those of us eagerly awaiting a Supreme Court pronouncement on the Second Amendment, for the first time in 66 years, the Constitution is on our side.

> *"Federal and state courts unanimously have held that the Second Amendment guarantees a right to be armed only to persons using the arms in service to an organized state militia."*

The Second Amendment Guarantees a Collective Right, Not an Individual Right

Legal Action Project

The Legal Action Project of the Brady Center to Prevent Gun Violence (LAP) files lawsuits on behalf of victims of gun violence against gun manufacturers, owners, or sellers. In the following viewpoint, the LAP contends that the widely believed assertion that the Second Amendment guarantees an individual right to keep and bear arms is a myth. The Second Amendment clearly states that it is for a "well-regulated" militia, the author asserts, and, according to the Supreme Court, the Second Amendment's "obvious purpose" was to guarantee the existence of a state militia. Furthermore, the LAP argues, the Founding Fathers were deeply distrustful of standing armies and of the power held by the federal government. The Second Amendment was written to

Legal Action Project/Brady Campaign to Prevent Gun Violence, "Exploding the NRA's Second Amendment Mythology." www.gunlawsuits.org/defend/second/articles/nra myths.php. Reproduced by permission.

prevent the federal government from disarming state militias, the author maintains, and therefore guarantees a collective right to keep and bear arms, not an individual right.

As you read, consider the following questions:

1. How does the language of the Second Amendment differ from that of the First Amendment, in the Legal Action Project's opinion?
2. Who were members of the colonial militias, according to the author?
3. What was the issue decided by the U.S. Supreme Court in *U.S. v. Miller*, as cited by the Legal Action Project?

How often have you heard the gun lobby and its allies respond to reasoned arguments for gun control with the claim: "Gun ownership is a constitutional right guaranteed by the Second Amendment!"? The assertion that the Second Amendment to our Constitution guarantees a broad, individual right to "keep and bear arms" is the philosophical foundation of the National Rifle Association's [NRA] opposition to even the most modest gun control measures.

The NRA's constitutional theory is, however, divorced from legal and historical reality. It is based on calculated disinformation about the text and history of the Second Amendment and systematic distortion of key judicial rulings interpreting the Amendment. This disinformation and distortion is disseminated by way of NRA publications and advertising, as well as by the persistent letter writing of NRA partisans to newspapers and elected officials. The result is the creation of a Second Amendment "mythology" which, because it so often goes unchallenged, has managed to penetrate the consciousness of many Americans.

The gun lobby must no longer be allowed to get away with its campaign to mislead the American people about the

Second Amendment. Gun control activists must be prepared to expose the NRA's distortions of the Constitution wherever they appear. . . .

NRA Myth No. 1

The Second Amendment guarantees the right to possess guns to the same extent that the First Amendment guarantees freedom of speech, press and assembly.

RESPONSE: *The Second Amendment was not crafted with the same breadth of language as the First Amendment. Instead, it begins by stating clearly its limited purpose: the preservation of "well regulated" state militia forces.*

EXPLANATION: The right guaranteed by the Second Amendment is far more limited and serves an entirely different purpose than the freedoms guaranteed by the First Amendment. This is evident from a comparison of the text of the two Amendments. The Second Amendment contains an expression of purpose which limits the scope of the right guaranteed: "*A well regulated Militia, being necessary to the security of a free State*, the right of the people to keep and bear Arms, shall not be infringed" (emphasis added). In contrast, the First Amendment contains no such similar statement: "Congress shall make no Law . . . abridging the freedom of speech, or of the press; or the right of the people peaceably to assemble. . . ."

In *United States v. Miller*, the Supreme Court wrote that the "obvious purpose" of the Second Amendment was "to assure the continuation and render possible the effectiveness" of the state militia. The Court added that the Amendment "must be interpreted and applied with that end in view." Following the *Miller* decision, federal and state courts *unanimously* have held that the Second Amendment guarantees a right to be armed *only to persons using the arms in service to an organized state militia.*

It is clear from the language of the First Amendment that when our Founding Fathers sought to create broad, individual rights, they knew how to do it and they did it very well. If the Founders sought to create a similarly broad "right to keep and bear arms", why did they include the phrase about the "well regulated Militia" and the "security of a free state"?

The NRA's distortion of the Second Amendment begins with its habitual omission of the militia clause when the Amendment is quoted. In fact, when the NRA placed the words of the Amendment near the front door of its former Washington, D.C., headquarters, the militia clause was conveniently omitted.

NRA Myth No. 2

Since the "Militia" in the Second Amendment consists of "the whole people," the Amendment guarantees everyone the right to keep and bear arms.

RESPONSE: *The original colonial militia did not include everyone. Rather, it included able-bodied adult males between the ages of 18 and 45. The militia was always an organized, state-sponsored military force, not simply an ad hoc collection of armed citizens.*

EXPLANATION: When the NRA is forced to address the militia language in the Amendment, it seriously distorts the nature of the "well regulated Militia." In the NRA's view, the term "militia" is synonymous with the general citizenry. The NRA relies on quotations from colonial leaders like George Mason indicating that the "militia" consists of "the whole people."

Membership in the 18th century militia generally consisted of able-bodied white males between the ages of 18 and 45. Thus, the militia was never composed of the entire population, as the NRA sometimes suggests. Moreover, to say that the "militia" is simply a collection of armed citizens is to misrepresent the original militia concept.

The colonial militia was an *organized military force* whose members were subject to various legal requirements imposed by the colonies and then by the states. For instance, militia-men were required by law to muster for training several days a year and to supply their own equipment for militia use, in-cluding guns and horses. (The personal arms of the militia-men were supplemented by militia arms from government armories.) The term "well regulated" in the Second Amend-ment reinforces the idea of an organized military force subject to state governmental control. In sum, the militia in 18th cen-tury America was a form of compulsory military service im-posed upon much of the male population or, to borrow a phrase from the late Chief Justice Warren Burger, a "state army."

A Distrust of Standing Armies

The Second Amendment was a product of the colonists' deep distrust of "standing armies"—permanent military forces com-posed of professional soldiers. The use of troops by [England's King] George III to compel obedience to the Crown's burden-some taxes and laws reinforced this distrust. These colonists saw the state militia—a part-time military force composed of ordinary citizens—as an effective counterpoint to the power of the federal standing army. Thus, the concern of the Second Amendment was the distribution of military power between the states and the federal government. *The purpose of the Sec-ond Amendment was to preclude the federal government from enacting laws which would disarm the state militia.*

In stark contrast to the organized military force that was the colonial militia are the private citizen "militias" that came to public attention following the 1995 Oklahoma City bomb-ing. These paramilitary groups claim a right to engage in vio-lent resistance to federal authority and assert that the reason for the Second Amendment is to provide the people with the means to resist the government when it becomes a "tyranny." These ad hoc collections of citizens who have appropriated the term "militia" are not the rightful descendants of the orga-

The American Civil Liberties Union's Position on Gun Control

We believe that the constitutional right to bear arms is primarily a collective one, intended mainly to protect the right of the states to maintain militias to assure their own freedom and security against the central government. In today's world, that idea is somewhat anachronistic and in any case would require weapons much more powerful than handguns or hunting rifles. The ACLU therefore believes that the Second Amendment does not confer an unlimited right upon individuals to own guns or other weapons nor does it prohibit reasonable regulation of gun ownership, such as licensing and registration.

American Civil Liberties Union, "Gun Control," March 4, 2002.

nized colonial militia of the 18th century. They are in no sense "well regulated" by the states; nor are they an instrument of state-controlled force. In fact, many states actually have laws that prohibit the formation of private military organizations like these groups (e.g. California, Idaho, Texas).

In the twentieth century, we no longer have "state armies" in which a large portion of the population is enrolled for military service and required to maintain private arms to be used in such service. The modern "well regulated Militia" is the National Guard, a state-organized military force made up of ordinary citizens serving as part-time soldiers. The arms used by the National Guard are, of course, not privately-owned, but are supplied by the government. Courts have consistently held that gun control laws affecting the private ownership, sale and use of firearms do not violate the Second Amendment *because such laws do not adversely affect the arming of a "well regulated Militia," i.e. the National Guard.*

NRA Myth No. 3

Current federal statutes indicate that the "Militia" protected by the Second Amendment is not restricted to the National Guard.

RESPONSE: *Federal law distinguishes between the organized militia (the National Guard) and the unorganized militia. The Second Amendment right to bear arms belongs to the organized or, to use its own words, "well regulated" militia.*

EXPLANATION: In making this argument, the NRA relies on Title 10, Section 311 of the United States Code (adopted in 1906), which defines the "militia of the United States" as follows:

> ... all able bodied males at least 17 years of age and, [with certain exceptions], under 45 years of age who are, or who have made a declaration of intention to become, citizens of the United States and ... female citizens of the United States who are commissioned officers of the National Guard.

Section 311 also distinguishes between the "organized militia, which consists of the National Guard and the Naval Militia" and the "unorganized militia," which consists of all members of the militia not members of the National Guard and the Naval Militia.

Two Problems

Based on these definitions, the NRA argues that every member of the unorganized militia has a constitutional right to possess guns under the Second Amendment. This argument has two problems.

First, if this argument were valid, it would mean that almost all women and all men over the age of 45 do not have a constitutional right to be armed. The NRA, of course, is not willing to take this position, since it would be inconsistent with the organization's view that all law-abiding, adult citizens have the right to be armed.

Second, the distinction between the "organized" and "unorganized" militia in [Title] 10 [Sec.] 311 actually cuts *against* the NRA's argument. What is the *well regulated* Militia" protected by the Second Amendment? Since only members of an "organized" militia are by definition "well regulated" in their militia service, clearly it is *that* militia that is protected by the Second Amendment.

Only the "organized" modern militia bears any resemblance to the militia in existence in 1791 when the Bill of Rights was adopted. There was no "unorganized" militia in 1791.... The militia of 1791 was a military force subject to a set of regulations to ensure that it was well-trained and well-equipped. Consider the definition of the term "militia" in Noah Webster's Dictionary of 1828:

> The militia of a country are the able bodied men organized into companies, regiments and brigades, with officers of all grades, and required by law to attend military exercises on certain days only, but at other times left to pursue their usual occupations.

The next time an NRA member claims a right to bear arms as part of the constitutionally-protected "militia," you might ask what company he or she belongs to and who is his or her commanding officer!

NRA Myth No. 4

In *U.S. v. Miller*, the Supreme Court decided that any gun that could be useful to a militia is constitutionally-protected.

RESPONSE: *Possession of a weapon is not constitutionally-protected simply because it could in some scenario be used by the state militia. Rather, the possession and use of the weapon must be connected with active service in the state militia.*

EXPLANATION: The Supreme Court's opinion in *U.S. v. Miller*, is its most extensive discussion of the Second Amendment. The issue in *Miller* was whether the Second Amendment barred the prosecution of two individuals for transporting in interstate commerce a sawed-off shotgun that had not been registered as required by the National Firearms Act of 1934. As explained above, the Court in *Miller* held that the Second Amendment must be interpreted in light of its stated purpose to protect the state militia. In holding that the indictments of the two defendants did not violate the Second Amendment, the Court wrote:

> . . . in the absence of any evidence tending to show that possession or use of a [sawed-off shotgun] at this time has some reasonable relationship to the preservation or efficiency of a well regulated militia, we cannot say that the Second Amendment guarantees the right to keep and bear such an instrument.

The Court went on to say that it simply could not conclude, without evidence, "that this weapon is any part of the ordinary military equipment or that its use could contribute to the common defense."

The NRA reads this to mean that any weapon which *can* be shown to be "part of ordinary military equipment" or which "could contribute to the common defense" is constitutionally-protected and cannot be banned. This position, of course, is absurd. It would mean that the government could not ban civilian ownership of machine guns, hand grenades, bazookas, rocket launchers, or even nuclear weapons!

The Supreme Court in no way endorsed such a ridiculous view in *U.S. v. Miller*. The Court *did* rule that, in order to receive constitutional protection, a gun must have "a reasonable relationship to the preservation or efficiency of a well regulated militia." Obviously, a gun cannot have such a relationship unless it is possessed by a member of the "well regulated militia" in connection with his or her militia duties. Thus, the present-day possession of an assault rifle, for example, by someone with no connection to the National Guard (or by a guardsman for his private use) does not contribute to the preservation or efficiency of a "well regulated militia."

In short, although the *Miller* ruling suggests that, in order to be constitutionally-protected, it is *necessary* that the weapon could be useful to a militia, the ruling does not hold that such theoretical militia utility is in itself *sufficient* to confer constitutional protection, regardless of whether the person possessing the weapon is using it in connection with militia service. . . .

NRA Myth No. 5

The authors of the Constitution clearly stated their intention that the Second Amendment protect the possession of arms, even absent a connection with the militia.

RESPONSE: *Both the text and the history of the Second Amendment support the militia interpretation. The NRA consistently quotes colonial leaders out of context. There is sufficient historical evidence to show that the basic concern of these leaders in the drafting and passage of the Amendment was the preservation and efficiency of state militia forces.*

EXPLANATION: The NRA is fond of quoting various colonial leaders praising guns and gun ownership. There is no question that many of the Founding Fathers liked guns and praised shooting activities. Many of them liked pets too; this hardly means there is a constitutional right to pet ownership. The best indication of their intent in writing the Second Amendment is the text of the Amendment itself, which, as discussed above, clearly links the "right to keep and bear arms" to the "well regulated Militia."

In addition, the language of the Second Amendment, both as originally proposed by James Madison and as ultimately adopted, is military in nature. For example, to "bear arms" is a military term. People generally do not use this term when discussing hunting or sport. And, as originally drafted, the Amendment contained a reference to exempting "religiously scrupulous" persons from being forced to bear arms. Clearly, in including such an exemption, Madison was not contemplating disallowing those who oppose war from using guns for hunting or sport.

Moreover, many of the quotes used by the NRA are taken out of context. For example, the NRA likes to quote James Madison (the author of the Bill of Rights), who referred in *The Federalist*, #46, to "the advantage of being armed, which the Americans possess over the people of almost every other nation. . . ." Actually, that quotation is contained in a passage arguing that the state militia (then composed of most male citizens) will be an effective counterpoint to the power of the federal standing army. Madison speaks of the militia as a military force "conducted by [state] governments" by which "the militia officers are appointed. . . ." Thus, Madison saw the militia as the military instrument of state government, not simply as a collection of unorganized, privately-armed citizens.

Another favorite NRA quotation is from Patrick Henry: "The great object is, that every man be armed. . . ." Again, the quote is taken out of context. It appears in a passage of the Virginia debates over the ratification of the Constitution in which Henry is objecting to the Constitution as it existed prior to the adoption of the Bill of Rights. He is objecting on the ground that the Constitution grants to the federal government the exclusive right to arm the militia. Following the language quoted above is the following passage:

> . . . necessary as it is to have arms, and though our [Virginia] Assembly has, by a succession of laws for many years, endeavored to have the militia completely armed, it is still far from being the case. *When this power is given up to Congress without limitation or bounds, how will your militia be armed?* (emphasis added)

Thus, when Henry spoke of "the . . . object . . . that every man be armed . . . ," he was talking about the arming of the militia. Moreover, he took it for granted that the arming of the militia was a responsibility of state government, a view at odds with the NRA's interpretation.

| *"Every right is subject to reasonable regulation, and guns are no exception."*

The Second Amendment Permits Reasonable Regulations on Gun Ownership

Saul Cornell, interviewed by Scott Vogel

Saul Cornell, a historian, is the author of A Well-Regulated Militia: The Founding Fathers and the Origins of Gun Control in America. *The following viewpoint is excerpted from an interview he had with Scott Vogel, senior editor of BuzzFlash, an online liberal news magazine. Cornell asserts that guns have been regulated in America for as long as there have been guns in this country. He contends that the Founding Fathers were fearful of a national standing army, so they established local and state militias to defend the country if necessary. But, Cornell maintains, in so doing, another, unanticipated problem developed: a gun violence epidemic. In order to combat this problem, the states began regulating guns. Cornell concludes that the states can pass any gun control regulations they wish to, as long as they do not place any restrictions on arming militias.*

Saul Cornell, interviewed by Scott Vogel, "The Second Amendment Doesn't Prohibit Gun Regulation—In Fact It Compels It," September 4, 2006. www.buzzflash.com/ articles/interviews/029. Reproduced by permission.

As you read, consider the following questions:

1. What was the Founding Fathers' vision of the militia, as explained by Cornell?

2. What was the difference between a militia and an armed mob, according to the author?

3. According to Cornell, how did gun control change during the nineteenth century?

BuzzFlash: *Your new book,* A Well-Regulated Militia: The Founding Fathers and the Origins of Gun Control in America, *states rather directly that the Second Amendment does not prohibit gun regulation, but in fact, it compels it. Your research and conclusion is quite striking to a lot of people.*

Saul Cornell: The thing one has to appreciate in trying to understand the history of the Second Amendment is that we've had gun regulation as long as there have been guns in America. The Founding Fathers were not opposed to the idea of regulation. In fact, their view of liberty was something that they would have described as "well-regulated liberty." The idea of regulation, the idea of reasonable government regulation, was absolutely essential to the way they understood liberty. In fact, in their view, if you didn't have regulation, you had anarchy. Next to tyranny, anarchy was the thing they feared most. So it's really almost impossible to understand the Founding Fathers and their world view, including their views of guns, without understanding that they were strongly committed to the idea of regulation. What's interesting is that somehow this notion has completely dropped out of our modern debate.

You're saying that the contemporary understanding of the Second Amendment is radically different than how the Second Amendment was understood by the Founding Fathers?

Yes, that's absolutely correct. The thing that's easy to forget, unless you immerse yourself in the time period in which the Founding Fathers lived, is the great threat that they saw as a standing army. And against that idea, they developed this notion of the militia as a citizen's army in which all white men essentially would be forced to contribute their labor, their time, and indeed, to provide their own gun and their own ammunition so that they could take up the goal of public defense.

And of course, nobody in contemporary America, even the most ardent gun-rights advocates, literally believe that they should drop whatever they're doing at a minute's notice and rush off to muster the way the Minutemen did. I mean, that's how far we've gotten from the Founding Fathers' world.

The problem the Founding Fathers had to solve was this issue of a standing army. That was absolutely the one thing they did not want. And yet they believed that the country had to have the ability to defend itself—hence, the solution being the militia.

But later on, after they solved the national security problem, there was another and quite different threat. By allowing the prevalence of weapons and guns in the new country, they created somewhat of a monster, which was a gun violence epidemic in the cities—in Boston, in New York, in Philly, etc.

The Second Amendment was designed to solve the first problem, meaning how do we defend ourselves without a standing army? But in doing so, there came this other problem in the form of a gun violence epidemic.

An Unanticipated Problem

I think you've hit on an important change, an important historical development, that hasn't really been appreciated until the publication of my book, because nobody really delved into this.

You're quite correct to say that the problem for the Founding Fathers was how to create a well-regulated militia so that they would not have to have a powerful standing army. Of

Guns Have Always Been Regulated

As long as there have been guns in America there have been regulations governing their use and storage. Without government direction there would have been no body of Minutemen to muster on the town greens at Lexington and Concord. If the Founders had imbibed the strong gun rights ideology that drives today's gun debate we would all be drinking tea and singing, "God save our gracious Queen."

Saul Cornell, History News Service, *May 15, 2006.*

course, what they eventually realized is, in fact, they did need a standing army and you saw a push to reform the militia and to create a more effective professional army.

The second thing is, I would not call it a problem created by the Second Amendment. It's an "unanticipated problem" that the Second Amendment really doesn't help you solve. Once technology changes, and the market revolution engulfs America, then cheap handguns become readily available. Handguns were not a big problem in the founding era. They were relatively expensive and not very reliable.

Once you get this new change with handguns, and once you get this problem of interpersonal violence, then the question becomes: Can we get rid of this problem? What kind of laws can we pass? And basically most Americans and most courts conclude that the Second Amendment and the original provisions of the state constitutions about the right to bear arms really don't address guns like handguns—they're really about the guns that the militia needs.

So the question then becomes can you regulate, and quite strenuously regulate, handguns? Can you even ban handguns? And of course, the conclusion I found, generally speaking, is yes. The state can do whatever it thinks appropriate with regard to handguns. The one thing they can't do is pass laws which would, in effect, make it impossible for the militia to be armed.

The Founders did not want everyone to have full inclusion in the Bill of Rights. Some people had firearms, others were not allowed to have them. Some Americans were able to vote, others were prohibited, as we all know. One of the fears was a poor and armed populace. In terms of Shays's Rebellion, would you say that that event, more than anything else, transformed the Founders and their understanding of how to deal with the militia?

Anarchy vs. a Well-Regulated Militia

Shays's Rebellion is very important. For those readers who aren't familiar with it, this is an uprising in Western Massachusetts that occurs shortly before the Constitution is written, and really does rattle the Founding Fathers. George Washington, in particular, is really quite upset about it. Of course, what it demonstrates is that any time a bunch of farmers or citizens decides to get together with their guns and call themselves a militia, they're not going to enjoy Constitutional protection, because the Founders really were quite keen to distinguish between the well-regulated militias, which were under government authority, and an armed mob, which is how they viewed Shays's Rebellion.

So Shays's Rebellion is absolutely essential to understanding the Founders' view of guns and the dangers posed by guns, and the dangers posed by armed groups acting without government authority.

The modern myth about the Minutemen is that they were just private citizens who went out on their own accord. But the Minutemen were the well-regulated militia. They were mustered. Their names were listed on muster rolls. They trained. They were acting under government authority. They were not acting under the authority of King George, but they were certainly acting under the authority of Massachusetts. So the key thing for us to keep in mind is that the Founding Fathers differentiated between an armed mob and the well-regulated militia.

Gun Ideology in the South

The movement of a universal gun-rights ideology is rather twisted. In essence, modern gun-rights ideology was born out of pro-slavery judges in the South and radical abolitionists like John Brown in the North, each of whom embraced a violent ideology of self-defense. You write for example that John Brown is the bastard child of the gun-rights movement.

This was really one of the more surprising conclusions based on my research. There are two places in American law—well after when the Second Amendment was written—when you see something that starts to resemble modern gun-rights ideology later in the 19th century.

And the two places you see it are among the most radical wing of the abolitionists—people like John Brown, who basically were on a mission from God to end slavery, by armed violence. Whether it's trying to free slaves by seizing Harper's Ferry, or massacring slave owners in Kansas, John Brown really sees the right to bear arms as this God-given right, and as something that each individual can exercise according to his own conscience. That's anarchy. That would have been anarchy for the Founding Fathers.

Now on the other extreme, interestingly—on the other side from the abolitionists before the Civil War—the only examples of an individual right to bear arms comes from pro-slavery judges in Southern states.

And in just one anomalous case, they actually held that the right to bear arms, under state constitutional law, meant you couldn't regulate it in a reasonable fashion. This was rejected by all the other courts, but it's these interesting judges in the slave South who obviously think that it's important that everyone have a gun, because they're in constant fear over the dangers of a slave insurrection. So it's interesting that the two extremes of American Constitutional thought in this period on the opposite sides of the slavery issue find the clearest exposition of a modern gun rights–style ideology. . . .

Gun Control in the 19th Century

You write that in the 19th century, gun control became more restrictive, not less. Why was that?

Well, this was one of the most important consequences of my research. What happens within almost a generation, you start seeing a different kind of regulation emerge. You start seeing something that could really genuinely be called gun control. The laws are not just about safe storage. It's not about just the misuse of firearms. It really is trying to restrict the ability to use certain types of firearms which are perceived to be a particular threat to public safety.

The first kinds of laws are bans on the right to carry concealed weapons. Of course, permitting "carry-concealed" has recently been the goal of gun rights advocates, driven by the dubious work of people like John Lott, whose work has been now widely discredited. Historically, this has always been viewed as a bad idea. After these initial laws against concealed carry, states began to pass even more robust regulation, and in effect, banning certain kinds of guns.

So what happens is you get this new social problem. Legislators grapple with it. They pass laws. Some people challenge the laws. Then the courts get into the game and say, well, this has nothing to do with the right to bear arms.

And most of the courts come to the conclusion that when you carry a pistol for self-defense, you're not bearing arms. You only bear arms when you carry a musket to muster, or in some other militia-related activity.

Well, this is an important point because it's difficult to imagine being a congressman back in the 19th century, or even a

mayor, and watching your community be devastated by gun vio-
lence, and sitting back and saying, "Well, I'd like to do some-
thing about this gun violence problem, but, hell, I can't." I mean,
it just doesn't make sense that lawmakers would be prohibited
from solving essentially any problem, much less a gun problem.

I think you're right. I think there's almost no right in our
legal tradition which is absolute. Every right is subject to reasonable regulation, and guns are no exception.

There's been an effort among gun rights people to equate
guns with words. I think that's a serious mistake. I think that
guns clearly are very different than words, and have always
been treated very differently than words in American law. And
it's for an obvious reason—you know, sticks and stones may
break your bones, but guns can really kill you.

Gun Ownership and Gun Regulation

You say that we essentially have two histories in parallel order:
one, a history of gun ownership in our country, and on the other
side, a history of gun regulation—and they're not at odds with
each other.

Right. What I hope emerges from this book is that each
side in this debate, if they're intellectually honest and genuinely concerned about the common good, will recognize that
the right to own guns, although not guaranteed by the Second
Amendment, is deeply rooted in American history. For that
reason, I don't think anyone has to worry about all guns being
confiscated or all firearms being prohibited. There are just too
many guns in America and too long a history of gun ownership in America for that to be a reasonable fear. I think gun
control people really need to understand that gun ownership
is deeply rooted in American history, although not linked to
the Second Amendment.

At the same time, I think gun rights people need to recognize that gun control is also as American as venison pie, if
you will. Gun regulation is just as American as gun owner-

ship. Once each side recognizes that, maybe we can begin to move forward and find that middle ground which will allow us to enact reasonable gun policies that will produce the goals we want, which is to reduce gun violence.

> *"We are supposed to believe that 'shall not be infringed' actually means 'shall be governed by whatever laws and restrictions the state or federal government deem necessary.'"*

Most Regulations on Gun Ownership Are Not Reasonable

Jason Kallini

In the following viewpoint Jason Kallini, a regular contributor on Second Amendment issues on the KalliniBrothers.com Web site, argues that because the Second Amendment states that the right to keep and bear arms shall not be infringed, any regulation of the Second Amendment infringes on that right and is therefore unreasonable. Kallini maintains that despite having twenty thousand state and federal gun control laws on the books, gun control advocates still believe that the one law that will keep the streets safe from gun violence has yet to be passed. If that is indeed true, Kallini contends, then those current gun laws are unreasonable.

Jason Kallini, "Let's Be Reasonable," October 5, 2006. http://kallinibrothers.com/index .php?/weblog/lets_be_reasonable. Reproduced by permission of the author.

As you read, consider the following questions:

1. In Kallini's opinion, what does Saul Cornell believe the Second Amendment means?
2. What is the next "logical" step after reducing gun violence, according to the author's view of gun-control advocates?
3. According to Kallini, why do the gun-control advocates believe gun-rights supporters are "silly and pig-headed"?

With ... school shootings in the news, it's time for Leftists all over to start screaming about the evils of guns again. And boy are they loud this time.

I wonder what the reaction would be if every gun-rights advocate inundated news shows, political debates, and newspaper editorials with pro-2A [Second Amendment] messages every time a gun was used in self-defense?

But that's not really the point of this viewpoint. What I really want to point out are the ridiculous statements that the gun-control crowd trot out every time there's a tragedy for them to take advantage of. . . .

What you end up with ... are quotes such as:

Is there really a danger to our Second Amendment rights in requiring safety locks on guns to prevent their misuse by children?

and

The gun laws being proposed are not intended to overturn the Second Amendment rights of citizens to own and carry guns, and we find it hard to fathom that many of the restrictions being proposed would cause undue harm to hunters or gun collectors.

and "The Second Amendment doesn't prohibit gun regulation—it in fact compels it," according to Professor Saul Cornell.

Apparently, those of us who want an unfettered Second Amendment have been totally unjustified in our disagreement and skepticism of those who would take away our right to self defense. They're not trying to remove the Second Amendment. They're just trying to pass *reasonable* legislation to make it safer for all of us.

This condescending attitude is, I suppose, supposed to make us realize that we're just paranoid, *un*reasonable individuals who are allowing dangerous criminals to prey freely on society for our own selfish desires.

In fact, Saul Cornell would have us believe that the Second Amendment, *A well regulated militia being necessary to the security of a free state, the right of the people to keep and bear arms shall not be infringed,* actually means exactly the opposite! We are supposed to believe that "shall not be infringed" actually means "shall be governed by whatever laws and restrictions the state or federal government deem necessary."

And he, of course, preaches that

> At the same time, I think gun rights people need to recognize that gun control is also as American as venison pie, if you will. Gun regulation is just as American as gun ownership. Once each side recognizes that, maybe we can begin to move forward and find that middle ground which will allow us to enact reasonable gun policies that will produce the goals we want, which is to reduce gun violence.

and also says

> I think gun control people really need to understand that gun ownership is deeply rooted in American history, although not linked to the Second Amendment.

Silly gun owners, the Second Amendment was written specifically to control what firearms people are allowed to own.

The underlying value to all of these statements is that we're all on the same team, and that we all have a common goal—the reduction of gun violence. I don't believe that this is my goal in life, but if we don't start from this (false) premise, we cannot get to the next "logical" step.

That step being the need to pass "reasonable" gun-control laws, and "reasonably" restrict access to firearms for law-abiding citizens.

Now, what these gun-control advocates are implying with this second statement is that we do not have "reasonable" gun-control laws as of yet. That's why they accuse us of being so silly and pig-headed. Because we're preventing the *bare minimum* gun control necessary to keep our streets safe.

So, those 20,000+ gun laws already on the books, on both state and federal level? Those aren't "reasonable." The almost total gun bans in Chicago and Washington DC? The six-month waiting list in New York state? The three-day federally mandated waiting period required of every firearms purchase? The registration and licensing of all firearms purchases in states such as New Jersey, New York, Massachussetts, and others? The massive taxation placed on firearms purchases and licensing in many states?

Those don't count.

The inability for me to carry my firearm into a Post Office, or courthouse? Those don't count.

The required gun lock that is included with every purchase of a firearm? Doesn't count.

If I go out to eat at a restaurant while carrying a gun, and I walk within ten feet of the bar—even just to use the bathroom—I've just committed a felony. And that doesn't count either.

If mandatory gun lock laws to outright banning of firearms doesn't constitute "reasonable" gun control—and have no bearing on crime—what are we to assume constitutes "reasonable?"

I am open to hearing from any gun-control advocates who can explain this sentiment to me. I am willing to discuss the feasibility and Constitutionality of any "reasonable" restrictions they wish to place on my freedom to keep and bear arms. But don't expect to change my mind. We have had decades of gun-control laws that range from annoying to criminal to pro-fascist, and none of them seem to be solving the problem that they claim to be striving to solve. In fact, all they seem to do is infringe upon my Constitutionally protected rights.

I think it is time for the gun-grabbers to be a little more reasonable, and allow us decades to clean the books of their laws and see what ensues. I believe it is reasonable to take the Founders at their word, and assume that the Second Amendment means exactly what it says.

I'm just trying to be reasonable.

Periodical Bibliography

The following articles have been selected to supplement the diverse views presented in this chapter.

John Casteen	"Ditching the Rubric on Gun Control," *Virginia Quarterly Review*, October 2004.
Cato Institute	"Restoring the Right to Bear Arms," *Cato Handbook on Policy*, February 2005.
Amitai Etzioni	"Reasonable Regulation," *National Law Journal*, April 5, 2004.
Brian Friel	"Taking Guns Off the Table," *National Journal*, August 12, 2006.
Don B. Kates	"The Laws That Misfire," *Legal Times*, August 7, 2006.
David Kopel	"The Second Amendment Before the Court," *Liberty*, December 2003.
John R. Lott Jr.	"Hype and Reality," *Washington Times*, October 28, 2005.
John R. Lott Jr.	"The Road to Bad Laws Is Paved with Good Intentions," *National Review Online*, March 23, 2005. www.nationalreview.com.
Joyce Lee Malcolm	"Gun Control's Twisted Outcome," *Reason Online*, November 2002. www.reason.org.
John J. Miller	"High Caliber Advocacy," *National Review*, February 14, 2005.
Minneapolis Star-Tribune	"The Constitution's Gun-Control Pledge," September 23, 2006.
Dorothy Anne Seese	"Gun Control Is Unconstitutional," *Price of Liberty*, July 22, 2004.
Barry S. Willdorf	"We Don't Shoot You Here," *A Gauche Press*, April 14, 2005. www.agauchepress.com.

CHAPTER 3

Do Gun Control Regulations Reduce Crime and Violence?

Chapter Preface

Horrified by mass murders in the late 1980s and early 1990s in which the killers used rifles that were similar in appearance to military-style weapons, gun control advocates pushed Congress to outlaw the sale of semiautomatic firearms they called "assault weapons." Supporters of the ban argued that the sole purpose of assault weapons was to kill as many human beings in as short a time as possible; if the guns were banned, they contended, fewer people would die from gun violence. Congress finally passed the Assault Weapons Ban in 1994 with the stipulation that the ban would expire in ten years unless it was renewed.

Since *assault weapon* is a term devised by gun control advocates, Congress had to include in the bill a description of the weapons that were banned, along with a few specific gun models that could no longer be manufactured. According to the ban, a rifle that had a detachable magazine for the bullets, along with two or more of the following was considered an assault weapon: folding or telescopic stock; pistol grip below the stock; a mount for a bayonet: a threaded barrel on which a flash suppressor or silencer could be added; or a grenade launcher. Handguns had similar regulations, including one that banned the weapon if the gun was a semiautomatic version of a fully automatic gun. (Semiautomatic guns require that the trigger be pulled once for each shot: a fully automatic weapon shoots bullets for as long as the trigger is squeezed or until the gun runs out of bullets. Fully automatic weapons have been strictly regulated by the federal government since 1934 and the public may not legally purchase them.)

The Assault Weapons Ban expired in 2004 without being renewed by Congress. Those who supported letting the ban expire argued that the ban had had little effect on reducing crime. They pointed to the fact that assault weapons were used in very few crimes even before the ban. In addition, they cited a 2004 report by the Department of Justice that concluded, "The ban's impact on gun violence is likely to be small at best, and perhaps too small for reliable measurement." Furthermore, gun manufacturers made small cosmetic changes to banned weapons that made the new firearms legal to sell under the Assault Weapons Ban. For example, the TEC-9, a banned gun, had its barrel threading and shroud removed and was sold as the AB-10. The banned AR-15 was changed to the XM-15 by removing the barrel threading and bayonet mount.

The Brady Campaign to Prevent Gun Violence advocates reinstating the ban and claims that the number of assault weapons used to commit crimes dropped substantially after the ban took effect. According to the Brady Campaign, "As more and more assault weapons are confiscated from crime scenes, fewer and fewer criminals and juveniles will have access to these deadly killing machines." It notes in its 2004 report *On Target: The Effect of the 1994 Federal Assault Weapons Act* that the number of assault weapons used in crimes and traced by the Bureau of Alcohol, Tobacco, Firearms, and Explosives (ATF) fell dramatically: "Since the law's enactment . . . assault weapons have made up only 1.61% of the guns ATF has traced to crime—a drop of 66% from the pre-ban rate."

Supporters and opponents of the assault weapons ban continue to debate the effectiveness of the ban. Meanwhile gun control advocates push for more gun control laws, including a ban on .50-caliber weapons—firearms they contend are ideal for terrorists who wish to take down a commercial jet—while critics argue that such gun control is unconstitutional and ineffective at reducing crime. The authors in the following chapter debate whether gun control regulations reduce crime and violence.

> *"National, comprehensive gun laws . . .*
> *have proven to be successful and effec-*
> *tive tools for keeping the wrong guns*
> *out of the wrong people's hands."*

Restricting Gun Ownership Protects Society and Reduces Crime

Brady Campaign to Prevent Gun Violence

In the following viewpoint the Brady Campaign to Prevent Gun Violence (BCPGV) argues that strong national laws that require background checks, ban assault weapons, and limit access to guns by children and criminals, reduce gun violence. The author maintains that thousands of criminals, gun traffickers, and spouse abusers have been prevented from buying guns because of required background checks. In addition, the organization asserts, the assault weapons ban reduced the number of assault weapons used to commit crimes; however, until the loopholes in the nation's gun laws are closed, criminals and children will still be able to easily acquire guns, it argues. BCPGV is the nation's largest organization dedicated to enacting and enforcing gun control laws.

Brady Campaign to Prevent Gun Violence, "Gun Laws Work, Loopholes Don't." www .bradycampaign.org. Reproduced by permission.

As you read, consider the following questions:

1. When was the nation's first gun law enacted, and what events spurred the passage of national gun control laws, according to the author?
2. According to the Brady Campaign, how did the Brady Law change how gun sales were made?
3. How many felons and other prohibited purchasers were stopped from buying handguns during the first six years of the Brady Law, according to the author?

D o gun laws work? Yes. Despite claims by the gun lobby that most gun laws are unnecessary and ineffective at preventing gun violence, our gun laws do work. While the Brady Campaign recognizes that gun control regulation is not a cure-all for all of our nation's gun violence problems, national, comprehensive gun laws—such as the Brady Law and the federal assault weapons ban—have proven to be successful and effective tools for keeping the wrong guns out of the wrong people's hands. By 2000, violent crime had fallen for six straight years, thanks, in part, to strong gun laws that provided mandatory background checks, banned the most dangerous types of assault weapons, and limited accessibility to kids and criminals.

But more needs to be done. In 1998 alone, 30,708 Americans died from gunfire. While our nation's gun laws have saved lives by making it more difficult for criminals, juveniles and other prohibited purchasers to buy guns over-the-counter, loopholes in our laws exist that continue to allow potentially dangerous people to get guns too easily. And even states with their own tough gun laws are victimized by the availability of guns in lax states. The tragic stories of gun violence that we read about or see on television everyday illustrate that current laws need to be strengthened, not weakened, and [these stories] expose the gaping loopholes in our firearms laws which enable minors—and criminals—to get firearms. These loopholes exist, in large part, because the gun lobby continues to resist any attempt to close them.

A Brief History of Gun Control Laws

Gun control did not begin with the passage of the Brady Act in 1993. Our nation's first major gun law was the Gun Control Act of 1968, which was passed in the wake of the assassinations of Dr. Martin Luther King, Jr. and Senator Robert F. Kennedy earlier that year. The 1968 Gun Control Act established categories of prohibited gun purchasers and possessors, including convicted felons, fugitives from justice, minors, individuals with a history of mental illness, anyone dishonorably discharged from the military, expatriates, and illegal aliens. The law also banned the mail-order sales of all firearms and ammunition, such as the rifle used by Lee Harvey Oswald to shoot President John F. Kennedy. The law also set standards for gun dealers and age guidelines for gun purchasers and prohibited the sale and manufacture of new fully automatic civilian machine guns.

The Gun Control Act of 1968 has become the foundation for our current federal gun laws, and has been instrumental in the ongoing fight against gun violence in America. But, until the implementation of the Brady Law in 1994, gun sales operated on an "honor system." A prospective firearm purchaser merely had to sign a statement attesting that he or she was not legally forbidden from purchasing a firearm. In most states, no follow-up was conducted to make sure the statements made on the form were true. Thus, convicted criminals and other prohibited purchasers could simply provide false information on their firearm applications and purchase a firearm despite being legally forbidden from doing so. The Brady Law changed this "lie-and-buy" system to a "background check-then-buy" [system] by requiring that every retail sale of a handgun be referred to law enforcement for a mandatory background check.

The Brady Law

The Brady Handgun Violence Prevention Act (Brady Law), which took seven years to pass in Congress, was finally signed into law on November 30, 1993, and went into effect in February 1994. In its original form, the Brady Law required a five-day waiting period and background check before completion of the sale of a handgun. Unfortunately, the gun lobby was able to weaken the Brady so that on November 30, 1998, the five-day waiting period for handgun purchasers expired. It was replaced by a mandatory, computerized National Instant Check System (NICS), which provides the information for criminal background checks on all firearm purchasers, not just those buying handguns.

The Brady Law Is Catching Criminals

While the National Rifle Association (NRA) likes to argue that the "bad guys" only get their guns on the streets in the criminal market, the Brady Law has proven that criminals do try to buy handguns in gun stores. According to the U.S. Department of Justice, during the first six years after the Brady Law went into effect, background checks nationwide stopped over 600,000 felons and other prohibited purchasers from buying handguns from federally licensed firearm dealers. What does this mean? Thousands of murderers, spouse abusers, gun traffickers and fugitives from justice have been denied purchase of handguns and apprehended because of the background check required by the Brady Law.

Some examples:

- Benjamin Nathaniel Smith, an avowed white supremacist, was stopped by the Brady background check trying to buy two Smith & Wesson 9-mm handguns and a 12-gauge shotgun from a licensed gun shop in Peoria Heights, Illinois. The computer background check showed that one of Smith's former girlfriends had taken out a restraining order, disqualifying him from buying firearms. Unfortunately, Mr. Smith was able to buy two handguns through a private, unregulated sale before he went on an interstate shooting rampage which targeted racial and religious minorities, killing two and injuring nine others. His three-day shooting spree ended on July 6, 1999, when Mr. Smith took his own life while being pursued by the police.

- The chief of the South Carolina Law Enforcement Division (SLED) noted that, as of early 1998, Brady background checks had enabled SLED to clear over 400 outstanding warrants and arrest 242 fugitives from justice.

- In 1996, a Northampton, Massachusetts, man, who was a convicted felon, tried to buy a handgun in Vermont using fake identification. After the Brady background check, the man was denied the handgun and later arrested. The man had recently completed a six-to-eight year prison sentence for burning the house of a woman who was a witness against him in a case.

- In 1996, the Brady Law stopped a handgun sale in Colorado to a man who was wanted for armed robbery in the state of Washington. Thanks to the Brady background check, he was arrested in Colorado and extradited back to Washington.

Helping Reduce Crime and Gun Trafficking in America

- According to an analysis of the FBI Uniform Crime Report, the percentage of violent crimes committed with firearms has declined dramatically after the Brady Law went into effect. What's more, gun-related violent crime is decreasing even faster than violent crime overall.

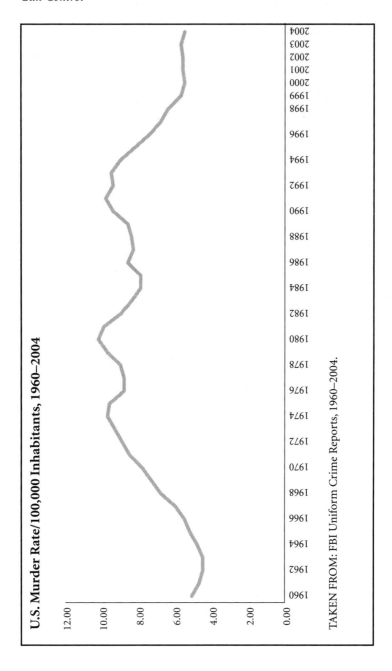

U.S. Murder Rate/100,000 Inhabitants, 1960–2004

TAKEN FROM: FBI Uniform Crime Reports, 1960–2004.

- Since the Brady Law went into effect through the end of 1999, the overall proportion of aggravated assaults involving a firearm fell by 12.4%. The FBI Uniform Crime Report for 1997 shows that gun homicides have declined by 24% since 1993; robbery with firearms, by 27%; and aggravated assault with firearms, by 26%.

- A study by the Brady Center to Prevent Gun Violence analyzed the Bureau of Alcohol, Tobacco and Firearms' firearms trace database and showed that the Brady Act has disrupted established gun trafficking patterns by closing off access to guns in traditional source states, or states with lax gun laws. The study provided important evidence that the regulation of the retail sale of handguns is an effective means of interfering with the illegal gun market—running counter to the old adage that only law-abiding citizens are affected by gun laws.

Taking Dangerous Guns Off the Streets

Do we really need military-style assault weapons to hunt ducks or even for self-defense? No. Assault weapons, including the AK-47, UZI, MAC-10 and the TEC-9, are high-power "weapons of war" capable of rapid fire shooting and the capacity to hold 20, 30 or even 50 rounds of ammunition. Assault weapons are designed with military features such as silencers, folding stocks, flash suppressors, barrel shrouds and bayonets which are ludicrously ill-suited for civilian use.

The federal assault weapons ban, which passed in 1994, prohibits the manufacture and importation of 19 of the deadliest assault weapons and the "copies" or "duplicates" of these weapons, and large ammunition clips holding more than 10 rounds. Traditional guns designed for the use of hunting and recreational activities are not affected.

Assault Weapons: Key Facts

Assault weapon bans work. In 1989, when President [George H.W.] Bush stopped the import of certain assault rifles, the number of imported assault rifles traced to crime dropped by 45 percent in one year. After the 1994 ban, there were 18% fewer assault weapons traced to crime in the first eight months of 1995 than were traced in the same period in 1994, and the wholesale price of "grandfathered" assault rifles nearly tripled in the first post-ban year. Assault weapons were used . . .

- To kill 5 children and wound 29 others in a Stockton, CA schoolyard in 1989. The AK-47 held 75—that's right, 75—bullets.

- To kill 8 people and 6 others at a San Francisco law firm in 1993. Two TEC-9's with 50-round magazines were used in the massacre.

- To kill 4 ATF special agents and wound 16 others at the Branch Davidian compound in Waco, TX, when the officers were attempting to serve warrants on the cult in 1993.

Although assault weapons comprised only 1% of privately-owned guns in America, they accounted for 8.4% of all guns traced to crime in 1988–91.

One Handgun a Month

In the early 1990's, Virginia gained a national reputation as a "source state" for guns used in crime in Northeastern cities. Virginia's lax gun laws and proximity to Northeastern cities with tough gun laws drew many gun traffickers to the state to purchase handguns in large quantities for sale in places like New York City and Washington, D.C. In July 1993, Virginia made gun traffickers' work much more difficult by passing a law limiting handgun purchases to one per month per person.

The law has been enormously effective. An August 1995 Center to Prevent Handgun Violence study found that after the law went into effect, there was a 66% reduction in the likelihood that a gun purchased after July 1993 and traced back to the Southeast from the Northeast corridor would have originated in Virginia. Based on this information, researchers suggest that a national one-gun-a-month law could reduce gun trafficking tremendously all across the country.

Today, four states—Virginia, Maryland, South Carolina, and California—have enacted one-handgun-a-month laws as a roadblock for criminal gun trafficking.

Loopholes Allow Kids and Criminals to Get Guns

Although gun control legislation has succeeded in helping limit illegal firearm purchases, decrease gun-related crimes, deter criminal gun trafficking and reduce overall gun violence, gaping loopholes make our current laws inadequate for keeping guns away from children and criminals. These loopholes exist largely thanks to the intransigence of the gun lobby.

Prosecutors and law enforcement nationwide have called for the closing of loopholes that allow guns to flow to children or criminals. The Brady Campaign supports new, common-sense legislation to build upon the success of the Brady Law and to strengthen our existing laws to keep guns from juveniles, convicted felons and other prohibited purchasers. To do this, we must close the loopholes that continue to allow the wrong people to get guns.

"If a criminal is going to break into a house, what type of town would he go to? ... A town with a gun ban."

Restricting Gun Ownership Benefits Criminals

Robert W. Lee

In the following viewpoint, Robert W. Lee argues against gun control by examining the case of an Illinois town that banned handguns in response to a school shooting. After the handgun ban was passed, a homeowner was charged with violating the ban when he shot a burglar to protect himself and his family. Critics of the ban assert that they have the right to defend themselves against intruders. Furthermore, Lee maintains, since police generally take too long to arrive to provide any help, homeowners should not rely upon the police to protect them. Lee was a regular contributor to the New American, *a conservative news magazine, until his death in late 2004.*

As you read, consider the following questions:

1. What sentence did Hale DeMar face for his failure to renew his Firearm Owner's Identification card, as cited by Lee?

Robert W. Lee, "Defending the Home," *The New American*, vol. 20, March 22, 2004. Copyright © 2004 Amerian Opinion Publishing Incorporated. Reproduced by permission.

2. How long did it take for Wilmette police to arrive at the DeMar home after the second break-in, according to DeMar's letter, cited by the author?

3. According to Gary Kleck, as cited by Lee, how often are handguns used in self-defense?

On May 20, 1988, Laurie Dann of Glencoe, Illinois, walked into a second-grade classroom at Hubbard Woods School in nearby Wilmette. Armed with three handguns, she began firing randomly at children, killing one and wounding five others.

Dann fled to a nearby home, where she took a family hostage. When police arrived, she shot a 20-year-old male member of the family in the chest (he survived), then killed herself.

Dann had recently lost her job as a babysitter because the family for whom she worked was moving from the area. She was under psychiatric care, and an autopsy revealed traces of the prescription drugs lithium (for treating manic-depression) and Anafranil (an antidepressant). Before going on her shooting rampage at the school, she had set several fires and had attempted to poison some people with arsenic.

The next year, in response to the tragedy, the village board of trustees in Wilmette approved an ordinance banning village residents from having handguns, with violators facing fines of up to $750. Earlier attempts to pass such a measure had failed, but in the wake of the Dann rampage the vote of the seven-member board was unanimous.

Responding to Crisis

The ordinance's predictable, if unintended, consequences elbowed their unjust way into the lives of Wilmette restaurant owner Hale DeMar, his wife, and their two sons (ages 8 and 10). Sometime between 11 p.m. on December 29, 2003 and 2:45 a.m. the next morning, someone entered the DeMar residence through a large dog door in the garage. The intruder stole a television, a Sony PlayStation, and a set of keys to the house and the family's automobiles, including a BMW sports utility vehicle. The thief then fled in the SUV.

Mr. DeMar, concerned for his family's safety and worried that the thief might return, retrieved a handgun from a safe, loaded it and tucked it under the mattress of his bed. The gun was duly licensed and registered as required by state law.

The brazen thief returned at around 10:30 p.m. that night, gaining entry to the house by using the keys he had pilfered less than 24 hours earlier. Mr. DeMar had just tucked his sons into bed when he heard the home security alarm go off. Grabbing the handgun from under his mattress, he went downstairs to investigate. Finding the masked interloper in the kitchen, he fired one shot. The miscreant, undeterred, advanced toward DeMar, who fired three more times. Two of the four bullets found their mark, striking 31-year-old Morio Billings in the left shoulder and left calf. Billings, despite his wounds, ran past DeMar, crashed through a living room window, jumped into the SUV, and drove himself to a hospital in Evanston for treatment of the injuries.

Mr. DeMar called 911, but the police had already been notified by the security alarm company and were on the way. They arrived about 10 minutes later, and soon located and arrested Billings at the hospital. Billing's wounds required surgery but were not life-threatening. He was charged the next day with two counts of residential burglary and one count of possessing a stolen motor vehicle. In 1997 he had been convicted of retail theft, and in 2002 he had been convicted of another home burglary in an affluent suburb of Minneapolis, Minnesota. His criminal record reportedly includes some 30 arrests, convictions, plea bargains, and/or suspended sentences.

Legal Gauntlet

With Billings in custody, authorities turned their attention to Mr. DeMar. Police confiscated both of his handguns (the .38-caliber Smith & Wesson with which he shot Billings, and a .380-caliber Llama Especial). Then prosecutors had to determine if the shooting of Billings was justified. On December 31 [2003], Marcy Jensen, a spokeswoman for the Cook County state attorney's office, announced that DeMar had indeed acted in self-defense and would not face any criminal charges.

The investigation also found that Mr. DeMar had bought his guns legally and had registered them as required by the Prairie State's draconian gun control laws but had neglected to renew his state Firearm Owner's Identification (FOI) card when it expired in 1988. Through his attorney, DeMar claimed that it was an inadvertent memory lapse; he had moved in recent years, so did not receive notice that the card had expired. Nevertheless, on January 8 Wilmette police announced that he was being charged not only for violating Wilmette's handgun ban (a misdemeanor), but also for failure to renew his FOI card (a felony). For the latter offense, he faced a maximum sentence of one year in jail and a $2,500 fine.

Mr. DeMar's initial court date was set for February 6 [2004], but before the hearing began Cook County prosecutors announced that they were dropping the FOI card charge. Assistant State Attorney Steve Goebel told reporters, "We are not going to revictimize Mr. DeMar. We choose to prosecute the real criminal here, the person who broke into this house not once, but twice." Goebel noted that the gun that DeMar had used to defend himself and his family was legally purchased and registered. He explained that the homeowner had only erred in "keep[ing] current [his FOI card], and we chose not to prosecute this memory lapse," since it would "violate the spirit of the law and be a narrow-minded approach." He also said that the decision not to prosecute was made after conferring with Wilmette police.

Several Wilmette residents had shown up at the courthouse to lend moral support to DeMar. One, retired contractor W.T. Egan, rhetorically asked a *Chicago Sun-Times* reporter, "If a criminal is going to break into a house, what type of town would he go to?" Answering his own question, he quipped: "A town with a gun ban."

There remained only the question of whether DeMar would be charged with, and fined for, violating Wilmette's repugnant handgun ban. Initially, it appeared that he would not be. The Associated Press reported on January 1 [2004], that "Wilmette police say a homeowner who shot an intruder during a break-in will not be charged with violating the affluent Chicago suburb's handgun ban." But one week later Mr. DeMar was charged with violating the ban. In a news release, Police Chief George Carpenter, a staunch advocate of the ban, claimed that "choosing to use a handgun" in self-defense when an intruder breaks into the home at night "actually reduces your family's safety." He added, "It would be unfortunate and potentially tragic to conclude from this incident that Wilmette families will be safer if they keep a handgun in their homes. The opposite is true. Wilmette families are in greater danger if they keep a handgun at home."

So how are Wilmette residents supposed to protect themselves? Chief Carpenter advised residents to "immediately lock the door to their bedroom and dial 9-1-1, which will connect them in seconds to telecommunicators at the Wilmette Police Department. These experienced professionals will keep you on the line giving instructions, and will ask relevant, important questions designed to result in a quick and effective police response. Your family's safety is far more likely to be preserved by calling 9-1-1, and allowing experienced police officers to search your home, than by arming yourself and searching your home in the dark without calling police."

Allowing Citizens to Have Weapons Cuts Crime

The indisputable conclusion drawn from Lott's research is that in every case liberalized right-to-carry laws have caused violent crime rates to plummet. It's not difficult to understand why this happens. As a whole, street thugs and other criminal opportunists are cowards. They fear an armed populace. And although violent crime will always be with us, the deterrent effect of a reasonable concealed weapons law does indeed benefit society as a whole.

Rick Daniel, Myrtle Beach Online, *August 29, 2006.*

Ludicrous Advice

That advice struck Mr. DeMar as ludicrous. As he explained in a letter published in the January 22 [2004], *Sun-Times,* "Three minutes after the alarm was triggered, the alarm company alerted the police to the situation and 10 minutes later the first police car pulled up to my home. . . . I suppose some would have grabbed their children and cowered in their bedroom for 13 minutes, praying that the police would get there in time to stop the criminal from climbing the stairs and confronting the family in their bedroom, dreading the sound of a bedroom door being kicked in. That's not the fear I wanted my children to experience, nor is it the cowardly act that I want my children to remember me by."

DeMar also recalled the police response to the previous night's robbery when the SUV was stolen: "[I]n routine fashion [the police] came, took the report and with little concern left, promising to increase surveillance. Little comfort, since the invader now had keys to our home and our automobiles. The police informed me that this was not an uncommon event in east Wilmette and offered their condolences."

Writing in the January 22 [2004], Munster (Indiana) *Times*, columnist Lee Enokian pointed out the irony that "police would not have been alerted to DeMar's firearm ownership if Billings had not broken into his home." Enokian added, "If the Wilmette police had captured Billings after the first burglary, then DeMar would not have had to shoot him."

During a January 13 [2004], village board meeting, Chief Carpenter again defended the handgun ban and his decision to file charges against DeMar. The next day's *Chicago Tribune* described the residents who attended as a "feisty crowd dominated by gun-rights advocates." According to the *Tribune*, "When the Pledge of Allegiance was recited at the start of the meeting, several members of the audience loudly emphasized the words, And justice for all." One attendee told the *Sun-Times* that calling 911 "is not going to be as fast as a bullet" when confronted by crime-bent thugs in one's home. "My plan A," he said, "is to call 911, but my plan B is to have a loaded firearm and put a bullet [in]to whoever breaks into my home. I'm going to protect my family, it's all I've got."

The Chief's Weak Evidence

Chief Carpenter told the concerned Wilmette residents that he would not condemn DeMar's actions, weakly asserting: "This resident's decision to use a handgun will not be criticized by me. This resident was in a situation where he did what he thought was appropriate." He then reiterated a litany of misleading anti-gun mantras also found in the playbooks of national gun control lobbyists, while ignoring (or perhaps being unaware of) the impressive research compiled by such scholars as former University of Chicago law professor John R. Lott, Jr. (currently a resident scholar at the American Enterprise Institute) and Florida State University criminologist Dr. Gary Kleck. Dr. Lott, in researching his books *More Guns, Less Crime* and *The Bias Against Guns*, found that firearms are used five times more frequently to prevent crimes than to commit crimes. Dr. Kleck's analyses indicate that Americans effectively use guns in self-defense up to 2.5 million times annually (usually without a shot being fired).

In stark contradiction to these findings, Chief Carpenter opined, "My experience is handguns create a hazard in the home. My experience is that handguns are far more likely to be stolen, to be used or threatened to be used in domestic situations, or to be used or threatened to be used in suicides" than in self-defense. But when Munster *Times* columnist Enokian contacted the police department, spokesman Officer Roger Ockrim told him "that he knew of no Wilmette police statistics regarding firearm theft or their use in domestic arguments, suicide attempts or accidental discharge within the village in 2002 or 2003."

What Next?

Based on sundry news accounts, most members of the village board appear to have little inclination to modify or repeal the handgun ban at present, despite the local and national furor incited by its blatantly unjust application to Mr. DeMar. Trustee Bernard Michna thinks "it's close to unanimous there will be no change in the handgun ordinance."

Mr. DeMar could end the ordeal by admitting "guilt" and paying a fine, but he has instead opted to fight the charge. On February 6 [2004], the day that he appeared before Judge Thaddeus Stephen Machnik for the initial hearing in the case, his attorneys filed a counterclaim against Wilmette, contending that the anti-handgun ordinance violates their client's rights. . . . [Both parties dropped their cases in December 2004.]

Meanwhile, state senator Ed Petka (R.-Plainfield) and state representative John Bradley (D.-Marion) . . . introduced bills in the Illinois legislature that would allow residents in communities that prohibit handgun ownership to nevertheless use handguns in their homes for self-defense and in defense of other persons. Rep. Bradley told the January 29 [2004], e-mail newsletter *Illinois Leader*, "We have a right to defend ourselves, our property, our wife, our kids. People here are pro-Second Amendment and interested in protecting our rights and families. I think it's important to send a strong message on this." And the February 11 [2004], *Sun-Times* quoted Sen. Petka as believing that "in circumstances like this, an individual should be afforded the right to self-protection, and no government at any level should interfere with that right."

In his January 22 [2004], letter to the *Sun-Times*, Mr. De-Mar asserted: "If my actions have spared only one family from the distress and trauma that this habitual criminal [Billings] has caused hundreds of others, then I have served my civic duty and taken one evil creature off of our streets, something that our impotent criminal justice system had failed to do, despite some thirty-odd arrests, plea bargains and suspended sentences." He reflected, "Until you are shocked by a piercing alarm in the middle of the night and met in your kitchen by a masked invader as your children shudder in their beds, until you confront that very real nightmare, please don't suggest that some village trustee knows better and can effectively task the police to protect your family from the miscreants that this society has produced."

> "A .50-caliber sniper rifle, experts say, would be more than capable of shooting down an airliner as it took off or landed."

.50-Caliber Weapons Should Be Regulated

Eli Kintisch

A .50-caliber rifle shoots bullets that are just over one-half inch in diameter and is accurate at ranges of over a mile. In the following viewpoint Eli Kintisch discusses how easy it is to buy .50-caliber rifles. The bullets for .50-caliber rifles are capable of piercing armored plating, which, he asserts, makes the rifle extremely dangerous in the hands of a terrorist, who could use it to shoot down an airplane. Therefore, Kintisch argues, .50-caliber rifles should be subject to the same regulations that govern other types of military weapons. Kintisch is a writer living in Washington, D.C.

As you read, consider the following questions:

1. To what military weapon does Kintisch compare a .50-caliber rifle?

Eli Kintisch, "Easy Shot—The NRA v. National Security," *The New Republic*, January 20, 2003, p. 18. Copyright © 2003 by The New Republic, Inc. Reproduced by permission of *The New Republic*.

2. What are some of the targets that a .50-caliber rifle can penetrate, according to the author?

3. What are the only requirements for purchasing a .50-caliber rifle in most states, as cited by Kintisch?

R ecently I visited Potomac Arms, a gun shop on the Potomac River in Alexandria, Virginia. Making my way past the samurai swords and shotguns, I found the 17-inch Anzio Ironworks .50-caliber "take-down" rifle—named because it can be disassembled in less than 25 seconds—on display. Another brand of .50-caliber, an ArmaLite, was available in the back, a clerk told me. Buying either gun would not be difficult: Under the Brady Bill, I'd need to show identification, after which my name would be run through a computer to check my criminal and immigration status. With a clean record, I could pay and take the gun with me—with no permanent state or federal record of the sale required.

An Extremely Dangerous Weapon

Many types of firearms can be purchased that easily in the United States. Few of them, however, would be as dangerous in the hands of terrorists. A .50-caliber sniper rifle, experts say, would be more than capable of shooting down an airliner as it took off or landed. Indeed, aimed properly, this weapon could be as effective as a shoulder-fired anti-aircraft missile, such as the one used by terrorists in an unsuccessful attack on an Israeli passenger plane in Kenya in November [2002]. But, whereas anti-aircraft missiles are highly restricted for civilians in the United States and decidedly difficult to obtain illegally, high-caliber guns like the one I saw in Alexandria are available at your local gun shop, at gun shows, or even on the Web. They're also relatively affordable: Security officials estimate that a shoulder-launched missile like the one used in Mombasa would cost up to $5,000 on the black market, with more sophisticated models going for as much as $10,000. A .50-

caliber rifle, by contrast, sells for as little as $1,250 at Potomac Arms in Alexandria. Incendiary rounds, which ignite on impact, cost roughly $2 apiece and are also essentially unregulated.

While a .50-caliber rifle is heavy, and would need to be positioned in line with a plane's path, it has the twin benefits of being accurate from more than a mile away and of doing a great deal of damage on impact. "Any hunting rifle is dangerous to an airplane, but a fifty-caliber would be much more effective," says Ken Cooper, a firearms expert who trains law enforcement and security officials in Kingston, New York. Gal Luft, a former lieutenant colonel in the Israeli army and codirector of the Washington-based Institute for the Analysis of Global Security, calls the .50-caliber "lethal against slow-moving planes." Both experts agree that a plane taking off would be most vulnerable to the guns.

When I left the gun store, I drove for ten minutes to a parking lot outside Ronald Reagan Washington National Airport with a clear line of sight to a dozen or so planes waiting at the terminal. I watched a plane scarcely more than 500 feet away from me take off and pass right overhead, exposing the undersides of its giant wings, where the fuel is stored, for several seconds. Cooper notes that, since .50-caliber rifles with ammo clips are semiautomatic, "the fifty can continuously fire and get off a large number of shots . . . even at an airplane going over a hundred miles per hour." Unlike a terrorist, I, of course, hadn't bought a .50-caliber rifle at the store a few miles away.

A National Security Issue

Fifty-caliber sniper rifles are a relatively new weapon, dating back to the 1980s. In World War II, the Browning machine gun, still popular today, fired .50-caliber bullets at a high rate of speed but with little accuracy. Equipped with telescopic

A Real Danger to National Security

Fifty-caliber sniper rifles are specifically designed to engage and destroy materiel targets on the battlefield at long range. . . . Armored personnel carriers, aircraft, rail tank cars, bulk fuel storage, and concrete bunkers are vulnerable to .50-caliber rifle fire at distances of 1,000 to 2,000 yards. Our soft civilian infrastructure—airports and the jetliners in them, rail cars carrying hazardous materials, and toxic chemical bulk storage plants—is even more open to attack by these rifles than its military counterpart.

Violence Policy Center, "Why Regulate .50-Caliber Sniper Rifles?"

sight, the modern .50-caliber rifle shoots bullets, one at a time, with equal power and vastly higher accuracy. Up to five feet long and weighing between 30 and 60 pounds, the gun fires six-inch-long, half-inch-wide bullets that can rip through a 3.5-inch manhole from 200 yards away. In addition to incendiary bullets, armor-piercing rounds are commercially available. During the Gulf war, American soldiers used these to penetrate Iraqi armor from as far as a half-mile away, doing so much long-range damage against one armored personnel carrier that Iraqi troops in the vicinity immediately surrendered. Fifty-caliber rounds can penetrate armored limousines, airport fuel tanks, and, presumably, the presidential helicopter, Marine One. "This threat is not a gun-control issue but a national security issue," writes the Washington-based Violence Policy Center (VPC) in a . . . study on airport security and the .50-caliber rifle.

The military acknowledges the gun's specific threat to planes. As pointed out in the VPC report, several U.S. Army manuals warn against the risk of small-arms fire—such as that from a .50-caliber gun—against low-flying aircraft, citing heavy losses from ground fire in Korea and Vietnam. And experts say airliners' large sizes means they would be easier for snipers to hit and destroy than smaller, fast-flying planes. Airplanes waiting on the runway are also vulnerable. A 1995 report done for the Air Force by the Rand Corporation found that .50-caliber guns give "light forces a portable and quite deadly option against parked aircraft." In the November 2001 issue of *Airman*, the Air Force's official magazine, an article on anti-sniper efforts described planes parked on a fully protected U.S. airbase to be as vulnerable as "ducks on a pond" because .50-caliber guns could shoot from beyond most airbase perimeters.

Manufacturers, eager for military contracts, have actually used the gun's effectiveness against aircraft as a selling point. Tennessee-based Barrett Firearms Manufacturing, whose 82A1 model is popular with armies around the world, as well as with some enthusiasts, has claimed in marketing material meant for the military that the guns are "capable of destroying multimillion-dollar aircraft with a single hit delivered to a vital area." In the 1999 federal trial of six men accused of a 1997 assassination attempt on Fidel Castro, Ronnie Barrett, the designer of the .50-caliber rifle and president of Barrett Firearms, testified to his gun's usefulness against commercial planes as they flew toward a sniper's nest. Asked what he deemed the difficulty of hitting a landing airplane with a .50-caliber rifle, he replied, "Just like bird-hunting."

Lax Regulations

Right now, .50-caliber guns are subject to the same lax federal regulations as hunting shotguns or smaller-target rifles. In most states, the purchaser needs only to have a driver's license, be at least 18 years old, and have a clean criminal and immigration record. Fifty-caliber ammunition, like any other kind of ammo for legal guns, is also widely available: Congress has put limits on armor-penetrating ammunition for handguns, but no limits exist for any but the most lethal .50-caliber ammo. A number of Internet sites offer incendiary and armor-piercing bullets through the mail, and a 1999 General Accounting Office investigation found dealers around the country who would sell the ammunition over the telephone, even to buyers who asked about the bullets' effectiveness against ballistic glass or armored limos.

Part of the reason is that, while .50-caliber rifles were developed more than 15 years ago, their use has been limited to a small cadre of shooting enthusiasts who use the gun for long-distance target shooting or hunting. But the guns are gaining in popularity. Accurate numbers of the guns manufactured in the United States are hard to come by, but *Forbes* magazine says two dozen manufacturers now make the weapon, and gun magazines have in recent years reported on the burgeoning area of sales to military, police, and civilian markets.

In 1999, after VPC released a report on the gun's increasing popularity, Congress examined the issue for the first time. Since that year, California Democratic Representative Henry Waxman and a handful of other [Capitol] Hill liberals have held hearings and introduced legislation on the guns, calling for .50-caliber rifles to be regulated under the National Firearms Act. That law requires citizens to pay a licensing tax, undergo an extensive check, and wait 90 days to buy machine guns and other kinds of military weapons. This legislation never even received a committee hearing in the Republican-controlled House.

The NRA's Role

The National Rifle Association's (NRA) arguments against restricting these guns are less than persuasive. "They're used for target shooting," said Chuck Michel, attorney for the California Rifle and Pistol Association, Inc. (CRPA), the NRA's official state association in California. The NRA also claimed, in

Signe Wilkinson Editorial Cartoon © 2002 Signe Wilkinson. All rights reserved. Used with permission of Signe Wilkinson and the Washington Post Writers Group in conjunction with the Cartoonist Group. Printed originally in the *Philadelphia Daily News*.

an August 28, 2001, fact sheet, that ".50 caliber rifles are not used in crimes," ignoring cases of use by IRA snipers, drug runners, and cult members. In addition, they argued that the cost and size of these weapons make them unappealing for ordinary buyers, despite the gun's growing popularity among, well, ordinary individual buyers. "[T]hey're way too expensive and cumbersome for run-of-the-mill lowlifes," the fact sheet said.

Despite the flimsiness of its arguments, the NRA has successfully blocked the regulation of .50-caliber weapons on the state level. In February 2002, California Assemblyman Paul Koretz introduced a bill to regulate the weapons as assault rifles, and, given California's past success in passing other gun-control legislation, the measure seemed likely to pass. But the CRPA joined with an NRA lobbyist, local gun groups, and Barrett himself to oppose the bill, which died in committee. (One gun-control advocate suggested that pressure to kill the bill also came from California Governor Gray Davis, who didn't want a controversial bill on his desk as he ran for reelection.) Measures that would tighten regulations on .50-

caliber guns have similarly gone nowhere in the Illinois and New York legislatures, though the city council in Los Angeles and the Maryland legislature have successfully controlled or banned .50-caliber guns.

Ultimately, though, state regulation wouldn't accomplish much. (A committed terrorist would presumably be willing to drive across state lines to make his purchase.) And action on the federal level has thus far been close to nil. A year ago [in 2002], in a response to Waxman's concerns about the powerful gun's use in terrorism, the Bush administration implicitly acknowledged the need to control these weapons. In a letter to Secretary of State Colin Powell . . . , Waxman wrote that State Department officials had told his staff that the administration had halted export of the weapons overseas, aiming to keep the rifles out of the hands of foreign terrorists. But, in what Waxman calls a "clear backtrack," State said in a subsequent letter to the representative that its action was not a permanent "change in policy." That's too bad. It would have been nice to think the administration cared more about America's security than about the gun lobby.

> *"The only difference between those .50-caliber targets of opportunity and any other rifle in private hands is a matter of a mere fraction of a millimeter."*

Banning .50-Caliber Weapons Would Not Reduce Gun Violence

James O.E. Norell

James O.E. Norell is the communications director for the National Rifle Association's Institute for Legislative Action. In the following viewpoint he argues that attempts to ban .50-caliber weapons are the opening salvo in the war to ban all rifles. The difference between .50-caliber guns and other calibers is minuscule, he contends. If .50-caliber weapons are banned, it will not be long before other, smaller caliber weapons are banned and confiscated, he asserts. And furthermore, the antigun lobby is using terrorism as part of a propaganda campaign to frighten the public into banning .50-caliber rifles.

As you read, consider the following questions:

1. What would have been the effect if Rep. Jim Moran's bill, H.R. 654, had passed, according to the author?

James O.E. Norell, "Only a .50-Caliber Ban? Don't You Believe It!" *American Rifleman*, vol. 153, May 2005, p. 18. Copyright National Rifle Association of America, May 2005. Reproduced by permission.

2. Why should American gun owners be concerned about the phrase "intermediate sniper rifle" during discussions about banning rifles, in Norell's opinion?

3. According to the author, what happened when England banned large-caliber guns?

The .50-caliber is being dishonestly branded as a "terrorist" weapon, supposedly because it's a hair's breadth larger than other rifles. The anti-gunners' language reveals their true strategy: to ultimately ban all rifles, no matter their size.

Propaganda War

With the stage set and direction provided by the radical Violence Policy Center (VPC), CBS's "60 Minutes" used its Jan. 9, 2005, show to vilify .50-caliber rifles. The CBS/VPC story line was that these guns are "too dangerous to be in the hands of private citizens." Right on cue, anti-gun zealot Rep. Jim Moran (D-Va.) introduced the ".50-Caliber Sniper Rifle Reduction Act" in Congress. [The bill never left committee.]

Moran's bill, H.R. 654, is a prime example of how the gun-ban crowd seeks legislation that outlaws many guns in addition to those they target directly. A ban on rifles with a bore of .5 of an inch also would include many antique and blackpowder rifles and a number of big-bore rifles owned by hunters of dangerous game. And that's only the tip of the iceberg.

In addition to a freeze on possession and transfer of all center-fire .50-caliber rifles, H.R. 654 requires guns now legally owned to be placed under Title II of the Gun Control Act, and be treated like fully automatics—for starters, owners would have to register their firearms and themselves; submit to photographs and fingerprints and undergo a rigorous FBI clearance process that could last up to six months. Moran's ban would prohibit any legally registered rifle from being bought, sold, given, traded or willed. "Reduction" is accom-

plished with the death of the registered owner, at which time the once-private property becomes the presumed property of the U.S. government.

This far-reaching attack targets law-abiding citizens, while being disguised in ugly hype about "heavy sniper rifles" and threats of "terrorism." The propaganda war is calculated to frighten the unknowing public and fool and divide gun owners.

The Future of the Gun-Ban Movement

The centerpiece of the "60 Minutes" broadcast—as with the core of the entire VPC anti-rifle campaign—is manipulating the fear that a terrorist could use a .50-caliber rifle on U.S. soil. But one phrase hidden in the VPC's phony terrorism hype should prove to America's gun owners that they need to be personally concerned about the ".50-caliber issue." The phrase is "intermediate sniper rifle," and it is the future of the gun-ban movement.

For a practical definition, look no further than your own gun cabinet or safe. If you own a Remington 700 or a Winchester Model 70, a Ruger 77, a Weatherby Mark V or a Savage 110 variant, or any number of common bolt guns, especially in a magnum caliber, you own what the VPC would ultimately have the government treat in the same category as a "machine gun"—or ban outright.

A VPC propaganda sheet titled "Voting from the Rooftops," that supposedly targets .50 BMG rifles, shrieks about "the severe and immediate threat that heavy and intermediate civilian sniper rifles pose to public safety and national security." Read that again, dropping the "heavy" part, and you'll see what the future holds for your tack-driving magnum big-game guns, varmint rifles and target guns.

The VPC demands that these guns—your guns—be brought under the control of the National Firearms Act. Failure to register your guns—semi-autos, bolt actions, falling blocks, Trapdoors, you name it—would become a federal felony. Needless to say, an unregistered "heavy or intermediate sniper rifle" would be contraband. And under Title II of the Gun Control Act, any infraction, no matter how innocent— say, transporting a registered firearm across a state line without explicit written permission of federal authorities—could bring a 10-year prison term and large fines.

Coming Soon: A Ban on Every Rifle

Don't believe that this "reduction" of firearms ownership by caliber will reach the smaller bores under the phony targeting of "sniper rifles?" Read what Rebecca Peters, head of the U.N.'s global gun-ban group, International Action Network on Small Arms, said about the .223 rifle used by the "Beltway sniper." In an Oct. 23, 2002, appearance on "CNN International Interview," she firmly set the parameters for her notion of an international "sniper rifle ban." In response to questions about the Washington, D.C., "sniper," Peters said: "[W]e need to have fewer guns, but the guns that are in societies need to be under better control. And that means that civilians should not have sniper rifles, or rifles that they can kill someone at 100 meters distance, for example."

Clearly, Peters is demanding a ban on every hunting and target rifle. At the same time, Jim Moran, Hillary Clinton, John Kerry, Chuck Schumer, Ted Kennedy—you know the list—claim that the big .50 BMG is the favorite of terrorists and assassins.

"Sniper rifle," like "assault weapon," is an utterly elastic, all-encompassing term. The word these gun-banners are really focusing on is "rifle." The gun control dragon always has a need for steel and wood, but it has an even more voracious appetite for Freedom.

This time, it culminates with what the gun control crowd always promised it would never go after—hunting rifles. The only difference between those .50-caliber targets of opportunity and any other rifle in private hands is a matter of a mere fraction of a millimeter or a fraction of an inch in the bore. If such a restriction becomes law, that will be the beginning of gun ownership "reduction" based on bore size.

England's Handgun Ban

If you think this is a stretch, remember England's handgun ban. In the beginning, when licensed gun owners fought to stop confiscation of their registered handguns, the government threw them a bone—it only banned guns of a bore size larger than .22. Honest British licensed gun owners turned in their "large bore" handguns for destruction. They were told they could keep their .22s in government-approved lockups at government-certified gun clubs.

Yet, that "bore reduction" gun control had barely been in place when British handgun owners were told the government was going to collect their registered private property from the approved armory sites—.22s suddenly had become "too big." The rest, as they say, is history.

That's "firearms reduction" by caliber. That's history. That's reality. That's where all this is headed—under the smoke-screen of protecting Americans from terrorists with big-bore rifles.

> *"States with the most comprehensive gun control legislation experienced on average one to almost six fewer gun-related fatalities than those states with the most lax laws."*

Gun Control Laws Can Reduce Gun Violence

Ik-Whan G. Kwon and Daniel W. Baack

In the following viewpoint Ik-Whan G. Kwon and Daniel W. Baack compared violent crime rates for all fifty states and adjusted them depending on how strong or weak all the state's gun control laws were. Most studies focus just on one type of gun control law, which allowed the researchers to determine the overall gun use environment in a state. Their results show that states with strong gun control laws have a lower gun death-rate than states with laxer gun control laws. Kwon is professor of decision sciences and management information systems and director of the Consortium for Supply Management Studies at the John Cook School of Business, St. Louis University. At the time of writing, Baack was a doctoral student in international business and marketing at the John Cook School of Business, St. Louis University.

Ik-Whan G. Kwon and Daniel W. Baack, "The Effectiveness of Legislation Controlling Gun Usage: A Holistic Measure of Gun Control Legislation," *American Journal of Economics and Sociology*, vol. 64, April 2005, pp. 533–47. Copyright © 2005 Basil Blackwell Ltd. Reproduced by permission of Blackwell Publishers.

As you read, consider the following questions:

1. How many people died from firearm injuries in 2000, according to the authors?
2. Which researchers cited by Kwon and Baack found gun control laws to be ineffective in reducing gun fatalities?
3. What are the six categories used to rank states for their gun use environment, as cited by the authors?

In 2000, almost 30,000 persons died from firearm injuries in the United States, more than the number of deaths from HIV, alcohol abuse, or drug abuse. This high number of deaths is despite almost 20,000 laws and regulations regulating gun usage to some degree. In addition, . . . emotionally charged cases such as the Washington, DC area sniper and the Columbine, Colorado school shooting have elevated the gun control debate to one of the central political issues in the United States.

Despite the emotional debate, few researchers have attempted to take a comprehensive approach to the topic of gun control, focusing only on single gun-related laws. It is argued that some of the mixed results on the effectiveness of gun control laws may be a result of a use of different levels of gun control legislations. Therefore, more comprehensive measures of gun-related legislation would make a valuable contribution to this debate. . . .

Research Background

There is a body of research that has found gun control laws to be ineffective in reducing firearm-related fatalities. For example, [Gary] Kleck and [Karen] McElrath claim that firearms "appear to inhibit attack and, in the case of an attack, to reduce the probability of injury (to victims)." Other research finds a theoretical link between right-to-carry concealed weapon laws and decreased crime or decreased felonious deaths of police. There clearly is a body of research that posits that firearms actually serve as a violence deterrent.

There is also a body of research that finds a clear link between gun control laws and decreased violence. For example, in a comprehensive study of this issue, [Mark] Duggan finds that gun ownership rates are strongly linked to homicide rates. In his work, Duggan links sales of gun magazines with gun ownership. After establishing and measuring the strength of this link, he then uses gun magazines as a proxy for gun ownership. This allows him to longitudinally link gun ownership with homicide rates from 1980 to 1998. Other research links gun ownership to an increased number of homicides and increased crime.

Duggan also criticizes the results found in [research done by John] Lott and [David] Mustard regarding right-to-carry concealed weapon laws. Lott and Mustard's work uses cross-sectional county-level data to measure the impact that the concealed weapon law has on violent crime. Their study finds that such provisions result in fewer violent crimes without increasing rates of accidental deaths. Investigating Lott and Mustard's results, Duggan uses his gun magazine proxy to see if right-to-carry laws result in increased gun purchases. His analysis finds no such relationship. He also analyzes whether counties with higher rates of gun ownership have decreased levels of violent crime after right-to-carry laws are passed. Again, he finds no such relationship. Finally, Duggan reanalyzes Lott and Mustard's study by using states, not counties, as the unit of analysis. When states are used, no relationships are found. Duggan claims that his analysis has "cast considerable doubt on the hypothesis" that Lott and Mustard made in their study. [Dan] Black and [Daniel] Nagin also raised issues with Lott and Mustard's results. Black and Nagin insist that the results of Lott and Mustard are dependent on the inclusion of Florida in the analysis. If Florida is removed, they argue, right-to-carry laws have no impact on the rate of murder or rape. . . .

A Comparison of Firearm Deaths in the United States and Canada

Compared to the rest of the world, the United States has fairly lax gun control laws. There are enough guns in the United States to have a gun in every home. Canada, by contrast, has much stricter gun control laws; guns are more difficult to obtain, every gun must be registered, and gun owners must be licensed. A comparison of firearm deaths for 2002 for the United States and Canada shows that the United States has a much higher rate of firearms death than Canada.

Total Deaths from Firearms 2002

United States	Canada
30,242	149

Rate of Firearm Deaths per 100,000 people

United States	Canada
10.5	1.85

Source: National Center for Health Statistics, 2003.

A Holistic Measure of Gun Laws

The existing research on gun-related laws has all focused on the effectiveness of a specific gun law, such as the Brady Bill or a right-to-carry law. This simplistic measure has limitations. With a focus on just one law, issues such as statewide differences in implementation, public responses to the laws, and interactions between the new law and existing laws are easily marginalized in the model-building process, and this may explain some of the different outcomes between studies.

In addition, another major problem with a simplistic measure in assessing the effectiveness of gun control laws is that the body of gun control legislation differs significantly from state to state. For example, Hawaii requires a permit to buy a handgun, and the Honolulu Police Department is responsible for granting and keeping permanent records on all permits. In comparison, North Carolina also requires a permit to buy a handgun, but local sheriffs grant the permits and the records are kept for only a year. This is just one example of literally hundreds of differences between state laws. In this complex legal environment, focusing on only one law in assessing effectiveness may produce incomplete and sometimes contradictory results.

In this study, a simple one-law measure of gun control is replaced by a holistic measure of state laws related to the use of firearms. This holistic measure is defined as a measure based on the analysis of the entire body of gun-related legislation for the states in question. The resulting composite score on gun control legislation is assumed to represent the overall gun use environment in a state, not just the environment regarding a single aspect of gun usage. It is hoped that the results based on this comprehensive measure will address more effectively this important social and legal issue and fill the gaps in the literature. . . .

Gun Control Legislation

This variable is selected from the publication *Gun Control in the United States, A Comparative Survey of State Firearm Laws* by the Open Society Institute in New York City. . . .

The purpose of its study on gun control laws is to rank each state according to the extent of its gun control legislation. To accomplish this objective, information on state gun control laws is weighted based on information published by the Bureau of Alcohol, Tobacco and Firearms, the National Rifle Association, Handgun Control, Inc., and the Bureau of Justice Statistics. The collected information is verified with local law enforcement officials in each state.

Based on the information so collected, states are ranked according to six categories: (1) registration of firearms, (2) safety training, (3) regulation of firearm sales, (4) safe storage and accessibility, (5) owner licensing, and (6) litigation and preemption. Positive or negative scores are given based on the presence or absence of each of the above categories. Each criterion is assigned a value between 0 and 7. For example, licensing and registration, important types of gun control laws, are worth seven points each. Handgun waiting periods are scored as no points for no waiting period and six points for waiting periods of more than three days. Since federal law mandates a background check on potential gun buyers by dealers, states receive extra points if background checks are more comprehensive. Points are deducted from states, on the other hand, if they do not meet the federal minimum age standards. . . .

According to [our results], states with more extensive gun control laws experience on average almost 3 1/2 fewer firearms deaths per 100,000 inhabitants than their counterparts ($p < 0.01$), with anywhere between 1 to 5.7 fewer deaths overall. . . .

A Unique Approach

This study used a unique approach to measure the effect of gun control laws on firearm deaths. By using a holistic measure, our research is able to more effectively address this issue than other studies. Multivariate statistical analysis reveals that it is not a single gun-related law in a state that links to the numbers of gun-related fatalities but rather composite legislation on gun control along with other socioeconomic issues. Our research indicates that states with the most comprehensive gun control legislation experienced on average one to almost six fewer gun-related fatalities than those states with the most lax laws. Gun control laws are a deterrent; however, they only address one aspect of individual behavior regarding the use (and abuse) of firearms.

The results of our study also indicate that a variety of socioeconomic and law enforcement variables affect the level of firearms deaths in a state. While the effect of police officers is only marginally significant, when combined with the violent crimes measures it is clear that, in general, high levels of criminal activity lead to more firearm deaths. Finally, socioeconomic variables are found to be significant indicators of levels of firearm deaths. Both the percentage of African Americans residing in a state and the unemployment rate seem to positively relate to gun-related fatalities. The above results indicate that effective social and economic programs can also reduce firearm deaths.

> *"There just isn't any hard evidence that gun control affects crime rates."*

Gun Control Laws Do Not Reduce Gun Violence

John Moorhouse, interviewed by Mitch Kokai

The following viewpoint is an interview of John Moorhouse, professor of economics at Wake Forest University in North Carolina, by Mitch Kokai of the Carolina Journal. *In the interview, Moorhouse contends that a study he did on gun control laws and gun fatalities found no evidence to support a relationship between the two. Furthermore, he asserts, it is a myth that states with strong gun control laws are undermined by neighboring states with weak gun control laws. Moorhouse maintains, however, that there is a relationship between high crime areas and support for more stringent gun control laws.*

As you read, consider the following questions:

1. What explanation does Moorhouse give for deciding to do a study on the effect of gun control laws on crime rates?
2. What factors did Moorhouse use in his index of gun control?

3. What is the contagion effect, according to Moorhouse?

Mitch Kokai: In addressing this topic of whether gun control reduces crime or crime increases gun control, you actually put together a fairly sophisticated study looking at crime data and gun-control laws across the 50 states.

John Moorhouse: Yes, there is so much talk in the media and in the press about gun control reducing crime that, like some other scholars, I wanted to take a systematic look at that and did so by trying to explain crime rates in the states. It depends on a number of factors, which we could talk about, if you like. And also, since states have different degrees of gun control, whether that made a difference in the crime rate. But do it systematically.

Before we get into the details of your study, this was sparked by hearing something on the radio that didn't strike you as perhaps something that had been well thought out or studied entirely.

Gun Control and Neighboring States

A spokesman for the Family Physicians Against Violence said on a radio program several years ago that even if a state had good and strict gun control laws, they could be undermined and made ineffective if an adjacent state had weak gun control laws. And so, I was thinking, as an economist, I ought to be able to test that hypothesis. The good doctor said it as if it were a fact, but I interpreted it as a hypothesis worth exploring.

So, how did you go about trying to test just how good the correlation was between gun control laws and the amount of crime?

Well, as I said earlier, I'm looking at, or looked at, crime rates by state. And there are a number of factors: demographic factors, economic factors and law enforcement factors. And I took those into account. Then I had an index of gun control,

Problems with the Kwon Study

[In 1997] Ik-Whan G. Kwon et al. published a study the purpose of which is "to statistically and empirically evaluate the effectiveness of gun control laws that have been adopted by state and municipalities." They conclude that "the multivariate regression results indicate that gun control laws and regulations do appear to have some impact on reducing the number of deaths associated with firearms." The evidence they offer, however, is rather weak. They find that only about 3 deaths per 100,000 are avoided when the types of gun control included in the study are in effect. In commenting on the original study, [Tomislav] Kovandzic and [Leo] Kahane argue that it has a number of serious problems, including the way the gun control variable is defined, omitted variables, model specification errors, and the interpretation of their statistical findings. Furthermore, in spite of the study's stated purpose, no information about municipal laws is included.

John C. Moorhouse and Brent Wanner, Cato Journal, *Winter 2006.*

which was constructed out of 30 facets of gun control put into six categories and weighted. For example, a state that had a five-day waiting period before you could take possession of a gun, they received a higher score than a state that had only a three-day waiting period. Also, [using] the index from the Open Society Institute, I looked at the degree of law enforcement of gun control. And so then I used the index as a measure of gun control. I looked at the demographic variables, the economic variables, the law enforcement variables, and then this gun control index, which allowed me to compare the degree of gun control in one state with another. And then we looked at the adjacent states and their level of gun control and constructed a measure of the so-called contagion effect.

Gun Control and Crime Rates

So, putting together this study, seeing this index of gun control, comparing that then to the crime rates in the 50 states, did you find any relationship?

I found absolutely no support that gun control laws reduce crime rates. And [as for] crime rates, we looked at property crime, violent crimes—ten categories of crimes—and in not one of them did we find any impact of gun control, nor did we find that there was this contagion effect; that is, that a neighboring state with weak gun control laws seemed to have no effect on crime rates in the primary states. So, we found no evidence that gun control, or its absence, had an effect on crime rates. But if I may go on, what we *did* find was kind of the reverse. In areas that had high crime rates, there seemed to be political support for more stringent gun control. And so we looked at using crime to explain the gun control index. We took into account some other factors, and we found very strong evidence that high crime rates lead to more stringent gun control laws. But subsequent to that, there was no impact on crime rates.

Political Implications

One of the political implications of your study would seem to be that the argument that you set out to test would lead some to think that, well, if we want the most effective control, then all the states should adopt the most stringent forms of gun control to avoid having this spillover, or the contagion effect, that you were talking about. It sounds as if your study would suggest that, no, that wouldn't have [made] any difference. You'd just have stronger gun control with no impact on crime.

Yes, exactly. There is just no support for this contagion effect. But you continually hear people talk about good gun control laws being undermined by the laws of an adjacent state. I had not seen any studies that really explored that in a systematic, statistical way. And our study, again, found no support for that hypothesis.

Scholars always like to have their studies replicated to determine that what they found is, in fact, what the patterns would show in repeated tests. Would you like to see other people perform the same or similar tests to try to find the same result?

Absolutely. There are interesting questions that are related to the ones we addressed, or addressing our questions in a slightly different manner. This is always welcome. I am not under the illusion that this is the final study that will settle all the debates. It won't. It's just one among many, and I hope that there are additional studies in the future.

But the bottom line is, based on what you know from your study at this point, there doesn't seem to be any link between gun control laws and the crime rates?

No, we found none. And I should mention that the results of our study are consistent with some studies done in the '80s and '90s that were pretty sophisticated. There just isn't any hard evidence that gun control affects crime rates.

Periodical Bibliography

The following articles have been selected to supplement the diverse views presented in this chapter.

Ian Ayres and John J. Donohue	"Shooting Down the 'More Guns, Less Crime' Hypothesis," *Stanford Law Review*, April 2003.
Timothy Brezina and James D. Wright	"Going Armed in the School Zone," *Forum for Applied Research and Public Policy*, Winter 2000.
Ronald Brownstein	"A Smarter Way to Control Outbreaks of School Violence," *Washington Post*, March 25, 2005.
David Codrea	"Safe Schools," *Guns Magazine*, February 2005.
Samuel Francis	"Gun Control Is a Global Flop," *Wanderer*, November 9, 2000.
Bernard E. Harcourt	"Nazi Laws Are a Poor Guide," *National Law Journal*, July 5, 2004.
Alexandra Marks	"Why Gun Dealers Have Dwindled," *Christian Science Monitor*, March 14, 2006.
New American	"From Gun Control to Bullet Control," June 13, 2005.
Debbie O'Hara	"The Tragic Results of Gun Control," *NewsWithViews.com*, April 27, 2004. www.newswithviews.com.
Woody West	"U.S. Gun-Control Laws Don't Save Lives," *Insight on the News*, November 10, 2003.
Stephen Young	"Terrorists Can Waltz into Gun Shows to Buy a Military Combat Rifle," *Chicago Sun-Times*, August 14, 2004.

CHAPTER 4

What Measures Would Reduce Gun Violence?

Chapter Preface

For three weeks in October 2002, residents of Washington, D.C., and surrounding suburbs were terrorized by sniper attacks that killed ten people and wounded three. Citizen tips led to the arrest of Lee Boyd Malvo, 17, and John Allen Muhammad, 41, who had dated Malvo's mother. During their investigation of the so-called Beltway sniper attacks, police discovered that the pair was also responsible for killing six other people in California, Arizona, and Texas. Police were able to tie all the shootings together after studying the ballistics of the bullets found in the victims. Each gun leaves its own distinctive marks on a bullet as it travels out the gun barrel. By comparing the bullets from each shooting, police investigators determined that all the bullets were shot from the same gun.

Gun control supporters advocate establishing a nationwide database containing ballistic information on every gun for sale to the public. For example, a gun's firing pin would leave a microscopic engraving on the bullet casing. This information would include the make, model, and serial number of the gun, and the gun manufacturer would enter this information into a database. During a criminal investigation, police would be able to use the ballistic fingerprint (also known as a microstamp) to trace the bullet back to the gun buyer.

Local, state, and national law enforcement agencies already use ballistic fingerprinting to match bullets to guns used in crimes, and the system has been effective in catching criminals. Supporters of ballistic fingerprinting argue that if new guns were included in the database, police would be able to solve more gun crimes and solve them faster. If ballistic fingerprinting had been in use prior to October 2002, advocates claim that police might have been able to stop the Beltway snipers before they killed so many people.

Gun rights supporters contend that a national ballistic database is really a gun registry to track who owns which guns and as such is a violation of gun buyers' right to privacy. In addition, they argue that criminals rarely use their own identification if they buy a gun in a gun store. Moreover, gun control opponents note, the ballistics of a gun changes over time, and the ballistics change the most when the gun is new. And furthermore, it is not difficult to deliberately change a gun's ballistics, or to even change a gun's barrel or firing pin.

Ballistic fingerprinting as a tool to reduce gun crime is just one measure that is being debated by gun control supporters and opponents. The authors in the following chapter examine other measures designed to reduce gun violence.

> *"Gun shows were the second leading source of firearms recovered in illegal gun trafficking operations."*

The "Gun Show Loophole" Should Be Closed

Americans for Gun Safety

Gun control advocates claim that a loophole in federal regulations allows unlicensed dealers to sell guns at gun shows without requiring the purchaser to undergo a background check. In the following viewpoint, the organization Americans for Gun Safety (AGS) contends that this loophole can be closed without putting gun shows out of business and without requiring lengthy waits for background checks. Best of all, AGS asserts, closing the loophole would make it more difficult for criminals to purchase guns, thus keeping Americans safer. Americans for Gun Safety is an advocate for responsible gun ownership in order to keep guns out of the hands of criminals.

As you read, consider the following questions:

1. How does the AGS respond to claims that background checks at gun shows would take too long?

Americans for Gun Safety, "McCain-Reed-DeWine-Lieberman Amendment to Close the Gun Show Loophole: What the NRA Will Say Compared to the Actual Truth," 2004. www.americansforgunsafety.com. Reproduced by permission.

2. According to the author, what is the flaw in the NRA's reasoning when it claims that only 2 percent of prisoners got their guns from gun shows?

3. Why is it unnecessary to give priority to background checks from gun shows, according to the AGS?

Senators [John] McCain, [Jack] Reed, [Mike] DeWine, and [Joe] Lieberman intend on offering an amendment to the immunity bill that closes the gun show loophole. Their amendment is nearly identical to S.1807, legislation authored by the four senators, and every provision of this amendment is either the same as or more centrist than the [Senator Frank] Lautenberg amendment that was approved by the Senate in 1999 by a vote of 51-50.

McCain-Reed-DeWine-Lieberman has a less restrictive definition of a gun show than Lautenberg. It also specifically exempts private sales from the home, sales between family members and sales between members of hunt clubs from regulation. It creates a new category of licensee who can specifically perform background checks for unlicensed sellers at gun shows so that checks can be completed easily and instantly.

You'll be hearing a lot from the NRA [National Rifle Association] about what is in the amendment. This document will provide you with the truth.

The Gun Show Loophole

What the NRA will say: There is no gun show loophole.

The Truth: Under federal law, licensed dealers must perform criminal background checks at gun shows, but unlicensed sellers do not [have to]. Thus, at thousands of gun shows each year—table A is selling firearms with a background check while table B is not. According to the NRA, "hundreds of thousands" of guns are sold each year at gun shows without a background check.

What the NRA will say: Background checks will put gun shows out of business.

The Truth: Seventeen states have closed the gun show loophole on their own. According to the *Krause Gun/Knife Show Calendar*, which bills itself as the "complete guide for anyone who attends or displays at gun shows," states that have *closed* the loophole host *more* gun shows each year than states that have left this loophole open (an average of 45 gun shows per year in the 17 loophole-closed states, compared to 41 in the other 33 states).

Background Checks

What the NRA will say: Lengthy background checks take too long for weekend gun shows.

The Truth: Thanks to improvements made to NICS [National Instant Criminal Background Check System] by Attorney General John Ashcroft, 91% of background checks take less than five minutes and 95% take less than two hours to complete. For 19 out of 20 background checks, "instant check" is truly instant. Of the remaining 5% that take longer than two hours, about one-third of these checks result in a denial.

What the NRA will say: Criminals don't get guns from gun shows.

The Truth: "Crime guns do come from gun shows. That's been documented," according to ATF [Bureau of Alcohol, Tobacco, Firearms, and Explosives] special agent Jeff Fulton. In a comprehensive ATF report on illegal gun running, ATF found that gun shows were the second leading source of firearms recovered in illegal gun trafficking operations.

Criminals Exploit the Gun Show Loophole

What the NRA will say: A Department of Justice survey of prison inmates found that only 2% of prisoners obtained their firearms from gun shows and flea markets.

The Truth: The 1997 survey the NRA cites omits the obvious flaw. The gun show loophole did not exist until the Brady

Top Ten Crime Gun Export States—Per Capita (ATF Crime Gun Trace Data from 2001)

All of the top fifteen states that are the leading per capita crime gun exporters have failed to close the gun show loophole.

State	Crime Gun Trace Exports	Traces Per Capita	Loophole Open/Closed	Gun Shows (2003)
Mississippi	1,772	64.0	Open	19
Kansas	1,157	43.6	Open	35
Virginia	2,489	36.2	Open	29
West Virginia	641	35.5	Open	46
Georgia	2,428	31.2	Open	69
Kentucky	1,226	31.0	Open	43
South Carolina	1,160	29.9	Open	23
Alabama	1,301	29.8	Open	43
Arkansas	723	28.3	Open	24
Indiana	1,684	28.3	Open	72

TAKEN FROM: Americans for Gun Safety, "The Gun Show Loophole and Crime," 2004.

Law passed at the end of 1993. Thus, any criminal in prison before 1994, or an inmate who acquired a firearm before 1994, could go to a gun store without having to undergo a background check.

Here are several recent examples of criminals exploiting the gun show loophole:

Thomas Timms was arrested in October [2003] with 147 guns, 60,000 rounds of ammunition, a submachine gun, a 20 millimeter anti-tank rifle, a 12-gauge "street sweeper," and a rocket launcher. According to federal agents, he had been selling large quantities of weapons at Georgia gun shows that have been recovered in crimes committed in DC, New York, New Jersey, and Michigan. . . .

Eric Barnes, a licensed dealer, was indicted on 179 counts in October [2003] for illegally selling firearms without performing background checks at Washington State gun shows, including at least one firearm that was used in a homicide. . . .

Tommy Holmes pleaded guilty in October [2003] for being part of a gun trafficking scheme that included a known felon buying "dozens of guns" at Alabama gun shows to sell on the streets of Chicago. Fifteen of the firearms have been recovered in the course of criminal investigations or at crime scenes. . . .

Gun Owner Registration

What the NRA will say: McCain-Reed-DeWine-Lieberman creates gun owner registration.

The Truth: Special firearms event licensees (those that are certified to perform background checks for unlicensed firearms vendors at gun shows) are required to keep the same records as federally licensed firearms dealers—no more, no less. Unless one argues that buying a firearm from a licensed dealer constitutes gun owner registration, then one cannot argue that this amendment constitutes gun owner registration.

What the NRA will say: McCain-Reed-DeWine-Lieberman requires gun show operators to register all firearm vendor names to the federal government.

The Truth: The amendment does *not* require gun show operators to submit a list of vendors to the federal government. Gun show operators are only required to maintain their own records of those who sell firearms at gun shows. . . .

Signe Wilkinson Editorial Cartoon © 2005 Signe Wilkinson. All rights reserved. Used with permission of Signe Wilkinson and the Washington Post Writers Group in conjunction with the Cartoonist Group. Printed originally in the *Philadelphia Daily News*.

24-Hour Background Checks

What the NRA will say: McCain-Reed-DeWine-Lieberman 24-hour maximum allowable background check is a smoke-screen.

The Truth: The amendment is very simple. If a state wants to place a 24-hour limit on the length of background checks at gun shows, it may do so once that state has its background check records in order. If a state chooses not to limit the length of background checks below the current three business days, it does not have to. . . .

What the NRA will say: McCain-Reed-DeWine-Lieberman gives no priority to gun show background checks.

The Truth: That is because it is unnecessary. The NICS currently operates from 8 am to 1 am seven days a week and 364 days a year. That is why 91% of background checks are completed in minutes and 95% are completed within two hours. The remaining 5% are 20 times more likely to turn up an illegal buyer than the rest of the checks.

> *"Fewer than one percent [of imprisoned felons] obtained the guns they used to commit their crimes at gun shows."*

There Are No "Gun Show Loopholes"

Orrin G. Hatch

Orrin G. Hatch is a U.S. senator from Utah. In the following viewpoint he argues that the gun show "loophole"—in which unlicensed gun dealers sell guns at gun shows without performing background checks—is a myth. All dealers who sell guns for a living must be licensed and perform background checks on the gun buyer, he asserts. Furthermore, Hatch maintains, only a very small percentage of criminals buy their guns at gun shows. To require gun collectors—who are at a gun show to sell one or two of their guns—to be licensed and perform background checks on the purchaser in order to prevent a tiny fraction of criminals from obtaining guns would be detrimental to the whole gun show industry.

As you read, consider the following questions:

1. What is the punishment for dealing in guns without a license, as stated by Hatch?

Orrin G. Hatch, Senate floor statement, "The So-Called Gun Show Loophole," March 2, 2004. www.hatch.senate.gov.

2. In the author's view, how would the proposed amendment create a gun-owner registration?

3. In Hatch's opinion, why is the idea that closing the gun show loophole will reduce crime rates preposterous?

I [would] like to speak about the amendment sponsored by my colleague, Senator [John] McCain, and the so-called "gun show loophole."

Based on some of the arguments I hear made by Senator McCain and his cosponsors, it is apparent there are some misunderstandings about what gun shows are, how they operate, and existing applicable laws.

Gun shows are large events that are open to the public. These events attract a broad range of people. They include collectors, hunters, target shooters, police officers, and those who serve in the Armed Forces. Gun shows are an opportunity for Americans—fathers and mothers, and their sons and daughters—to pass along a family tradition.

Exhibitors at these gun shows include gun dealers—who are all federally licensed—as well as gun collectors, hunting guides, target shooting clubs, and vendors of books, clothing, hunting accessories, and so on.

No Gun Show Loophole

Now, what federal laws currently apply to gun shows? Contrary to popular opinion, there are no special exemptions for gun shows. Anyone who engages in the business of selling firearms must be licensed, regardless of where he or she does business.

More specifically, there is simply no such thing as an "unlicensed dealer." In fact, dealing in guns without a license is a federal felony, punishable by up to five years in prison and a substantial fine. Congress authorized licensed firearms dealers to conduct business at gun shows in 1986 under the Firearms Owners Protection Act.

So, what happens when these dealers sell guns at gun shows? Have these dealers applied for and received Federal Firearms Licenses from the Bureau of Alcohol, Tobacco, Firearms, and Explosives? The answer to both is "yes."

Dealers are required by federal law to conduct a criminal background check. They must conduct a check through the National Instant [Criminal Background] Check System at gun shows, just as they would have to at any other location.

So if we pass this amendment, who would it affect? The answer is not surprising, but unfortunately ignored by the proponents of this amendment. The answer is: it would affect law-abiding citizens. It would drive out and shut down the gun collectors who buy and trade some of their guns at gun shows. They represent a fraction of the exhibitors at gun shows.

And remember, gun collectors are not gun dealers and may not engage in the business of dealing firearms without a firearms license.

Registering Gun Owners

Let me touch on an issue that many Utahans and I find particularly troublesome. If we adopt this Amendment, it will effectively create gun-owner registration. I want to make sure that my colleagues understand how this legislation, if it became law, would work.

Under the amendment, special firearms event operators would have to verify the identity of all participating vendors and have those vendors sign a ledger saying they were there selling firearms—whether or not any of the vendors actually sold a firearm. This requirement is a modest improvement of the original bill which, as introduced, would have required vendors to submit to the Attorney General the names of all vendors slated to participate in the gun show. Regardless of this slight change, it is clear what the sponsors of this Amend-

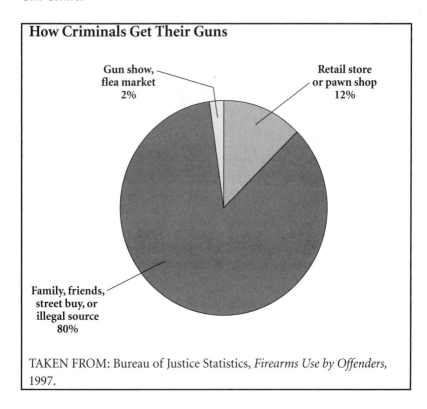

How Criminals Get Their Guns

Gun show, flea market 2%

Retail store or pawn shop 12%

Family, friends, street buy, or illegal source 80%

TAKEN FROM: Bureau of Justice Statistics, *Firearms Use by Offenders,* 1997.

ment intend. That is, to track and register law-abiding citizens who merely want to exercise their constitutionally protected Second Amendment rights.

So, suppose a private, law-abiding citizen enters a gun show hoping to sell or trade a firearm. This person, this private law-abiding citizen, would be required to place his or her name on a permanent ledger. Copies of the ledgers could be used for any future purpose.

Instant Background Checks

This amendment also purports to provide for instant background checks. Now, anyone who knows anything about the National Instant Criminal [Background] Check System knows they do not turn around such inquiries in 24 hours. In fact, currently, the National Instant Criminal [Background] Check System has three days to turn around a request for a background check.

The amendment before us provides that the wait may be reduced to 24 hours, if a state applies for the privilege of improving its records. With a three-business-day period still allowed to check out-of-state records, a few large states will drag down the whole scheme for all transfers across the nation.

Again, what is the practical effect?

Gun collectors, who occasionally attend gun shows for a day or two on a weekend, will be shut down because they will not be able to have the National Instant Criminal [Background] Check System run the required check on a prospective buyer and make such a transaction in that day.

Two Important Points Overlooked

There are two more important points that I think many of the Members in this body may have overlooked.

First, in November of 2001, the Bureau of Justice Statistics released a report on imprisoned felons and where they obtained their firearms. Fewer than one percent obtained the guns they used to commit their crimes at gun shows. And, of that one percent, only a fraction obtained weapons through collectors. What does this tell us? The idea that shutting down collectors at gun shows will affect crime in any appreciable way is dramatically overstated, if not preposterous. Criminals are getting their guns on the street or from residential burglaries, but not from heavily police-attended gun shows.

Second, and I want my colleagues to hear this, law enforcement and federal prosecutors continue to use gun shows to weed out corrupt gun dealers. In fact, federal prosecutors stress to me, passing this amendment would serve only to drive those few who would unlawfully deal in firearms without a license into the black market, into the back alley-ways, and into the hidden areas of our communities, making it nearly impossible to locate and prosecute such criminals.

So, not only will this amendment fail to address the true nature of the problem, but it will punish law-abiding collectors who choose to publicly trade their firearms.

A Negative Effect on Crime

I submit to you that adopting this politically driven, knee-jerk amendment, which only injects partisanship into a bill that otherwise enjoys broad bipartisan support, will have two effects: 1) it will shut down lawful gun collectors who attend and trade guns at gun shows; and 2) if it has any effect on crime, it will affect it negatively by driving the few dealers who are unlawful into the black market where it is exorbitantly more difficult for them to be located and prosecuted.

I urge my colleagues on the other side of the aisle to re-examine their analysis, put politics aside, and reject this amendment. It will serve no purpose in pursuing our common goal of fighting crime, but instead will only hurt innocent, law-abiding citizens. Let us not be distracted from the issue at hand.

We have legislation before us that enjoys broad bipartisan support and that deserves our attention. That should be the focus of our efforts—not passage of this unwise amendment.

"Membership on a terror watch list should not carry with it the right to bear arms."

People on Terrorist Watch Lists Should Not Be Allowed to Buy Guns

Steven E. Roberts

Steven E. Roberts, an author who focuses on terrorism and security issues, maintains in the following viewpoint that a terrorist with a .50-caliber rifle could do catastrophic damage to targets in the United States. He is concerned that no U.S. law prevents someone who is on a terrorist watch list—a list of people who are suspected of terrorist sympathies—from purchasing any type of firearm, including .50-caliber rifles. Roberts concludes by arguing that the Second Amendment's right to bear arms should not extend to those on such watch lists.

As you read, consider the following questions:

1. In the author's opinion, why does the .50 caliber rifle pose an undeniable threat to homeland security?

2. Why did California legislators ban the manufacture, distribution, transport, or sale of .50 caliber rifles in the state, as cited by Roberts?

3. How many firearms were sold to people on terror watch lists between February 3 and June 30, 2004, according to the author?

A t gun stores and gun shows in nearly every state, target shooters, collectors and the plain curious can readily purchase a .50 caliber rifle. Accurate at distances of a mile and as powerful as a small cannon, the .50 caliber rifle fires a bullet that will punch a hole through virtually anything. Armor-piercing or explosive ammunition—widely used in military settings to destroy armored personnel carriers or bunkers—increase its destructiveness.

Catastrophic Damage

Used by terrorists, the .50 caliber rifle could inflict catastrophic damage: An approaching commercial airliner, a rail car loaded with hazardous chemicals or a petroleum-tank farm would all be easy targets. For this reason, the .50 caliber rifle is now at the center of a heated debate, pitting legitimate homeland security concerns against the constitutional right to keep and bear arms.

Some state lawmakers have come down on the side of gun control. Effective Jan. 1 [2006] it is illegal to manufacture, distribute, transport or sell a .50 caliber rifle in the state of California. In enacting the .50 Caliber BMG Regulation Act of 2004, legislators found that the .50 caliber rifle represents "a clear and present terrorist threat to the health, safety, and security of all residents of and visitors to" California. Lawmakers specifically noted the danger that the .50 caliber rifle poses to critical infrastructure such as "power generation and transmission facilities, petrochemical production and storage facilities, and transportation." Citizens who possessed the weapon

Illegal for Aliens to Buy Guns

With a few limited exceptions, it is a federal crime for aliens temporarily in this country to possess firearms. Nor is there a plausible argument that this provision of federal law violates the Second Amendment, even under the individual right view. The individual right view, after all, repeatedly emphasizes the connection between, on the one hand, firearms possession for defense of self and country, and on the other hand, citizenship. It does not extend to aliens here on student or tourist visas.

Michael C. Dorf, FindLaw.com, *December 10, 2001.*

before the ban's effective date must register the firearm with the California Department of Justice.

Other states—and even the federal government—may follow California's lead. Lawmakers in Massachusetts and Illinois offered legislation that would forbid the sale of .50 caliber rifles. Introduced in the U.S. House of Representatives in February [2005] the .50 Caliber Sniper Rifle Reduction Act (H.R. 654) would take the prohibition nationwide. The federal legislation would make it "unlawful for any person to transfer or possess a .50 caliber sniper weapon."

An Undeniable Threat

There is no question that the .50 caliber rifle poses a threat to homeland security—and especially to vulnerable critical infrastructures. In a 2004 study commissioned by the Los Angeles World Airports—the city agency responsible for Los Angeles International Airport—security experts analyzed 11 likely attack scenarios. In one scenario, terrorists armed with a .50 caliber rifle shoot at parked and taxiing airplanes. Considering the effective range of the .50 caliber rifle, terrorists could hit aircraft from atop a building or a concealed location hundreds of yards away from the airport's perimeter.

The .50 caliber rifle already has been used against law enforcement: In the failed 1993 raid against the Branch Davidian compound in Waco, Texas, a .50 caliber rifle was fired at approaching federal agents attempting to serve a search warrant. Authorities had to call in heavily armored vehicles for protection.

However, the .50 caliber rifle debate raises a more fundamental issue regarding terrorist access to any firearm, not simply the most powerful ones. While federal law precludes individuals who have been convicted of a felony or who are in the United States unlawfully from purchasing a firearm, inclusion on a government terror watch list is not a disqualifier. Individuals who are currently on a terror watch list may legally purchase a firearm—including a .50 caliber rifle—provided the prospective purchaser submits to the appropriate background check and is not otherwise disqualified by law. This very scenario unfolds dozens of times each year in gun stores and at gun shows across the country.

A report by the Government Accountability Office found that between Feb. 3, 2004, and June 30, 2004, 35 firearm transactions were allowed to proceed, even though the required background check revealed that the purchaser was on a government terror watch list. Why these weapons were purchased or to whom they might be unlawfully transferred after purchase is unknown. Indeed, firearms bought legally in the United States by terrorist sympathizers could even make their way through the black and gray arms markets of the world to Afghanistan or Iraq and be used against American forces. To date, federal firearms laws have not accounted for this possibility.

Whether involving an ultrapowerful .50 caliber rifle or the comparatively paltry .22 caliber target rifle, gun laws must be amended to prohibit individuals who appear on terror watch lists from purchasing weapons. At a minimum, membership on a terror watch list should not carry with it the right to bear arms.

> *"A 'watch list' is only that. It is not even probable cause. If you had probable cause that these suspects had done something illegal, you could arrest them."*

Banning People on Terrorist Watch Lists from Buying Guns Will be Ineffective

John R. Lott Jr. and Sonya D. Jones

In the following viewpoint John R. Lott Jr. and Sonya D. Jones argue that prohibiting gun sales to people on terrorist watch lists—a list of people sympathetic to terrorist groups—is likely to be unsuccessful in stopping terrorists. Being on the watch list does not mean the person has done anything wrong, they assert. If the suspected terrorist sympathizer had done something illegal, the police would have probable cause and would be able to arrest them, the authors contend. Denying a person the right to buy a gun simply because he is on a watch list could lead to a slippery slope where other "undesirables" are denied their Second Amendment rights. Lott is an economist and resident scholar at the American Enterprise Institute, specializing in Second Amend-

ment issues. Jones is a fellow in the College of Public Interest Law at the Pacific Legal Foundation in Bellevue, Washington.

As you read, consider the following questions:

1. How many gun purchases were made by people on terrorist watch lists in the first half of 2004, according to a report cited by the authors?
2. Why were the gun purchases allowed, in Lott and Jones's opinion?
3. What evidence do the authors present to support their contention that background checks are not the solution to crime?

Should people lose rights because they are sympathetic to, but do not actually help, terrorist groups? Should law enforcement and not judges be the arbiter of those sympathizers who should be placed on "watch lists"?

In Senate hearings on renewing the Patriot Act, . . . Democratic Senators Ted Kennedy and Charles Schumer said the answer to both questions was "yes." Attorney General Alberto Gonzales and FBI Director Robert Mueller were grilled over a report showing that 35 gun purchases during the first half of [2004] were made by people on terrorist "watch lists," and the Senators called it a major public security risk.

Messrs. Kennedy and Schumer's proposed solution? Simply ban the sale of guns to people law enforcement places on the watch list.

Sensationalistic Fears

The *New York Times* also sounded the alarm with an editorial entitled, "An Insecure Nation." The *Times* could not resist further sensationalizing the concerns. Fanning fears of terrorists being "free to buy an AK-47," it failed to mention that in the worst case these would be civilian, semi-automatic versions of the guns (just like any hunting rifle), not the machine guns used by militaries around the world.

An Arbitrary Decision

The supposed link to terrorism provides a new possible reason to ban 50-caliber rifles. *60 Minutes* darkly warned of ".50-caliber rifles, a gun that can kill someone from over a mile away and even bring down an airplane" and that "the bullets blew right through the steel plate." But the decision to demonize these particular guns and not say .475-caliber hunting rifles is completely arbitrary. The difference in width of these bullets is a trivial .025 inches. What's next? Banning .45-caliber pistols? Instead of protecting people from terrorists or criminals, the whole strategy is to gradually reduce the type of guns that people can own.

John R. Lott Jr., Tech Central Station, *March 25, 2005.*
www.techcentralstation.com.

The 35 "suspected" purchases, out of 3.1 million total transactions, were allowed because background checks found no prohibiting information. No felonies or disqualifying misdemeanors, for example. They were neither fugitives from justice nor illegal aliens. Nor had they ever disavowed their U.S. citizenship.

As Mr. Mueller pointed out, the FBI was alerted when these sales took place, but the transactions weren't stopped because the law didn't prohibit them. But Mr. Mueller assured the Senators that "we then will pursue [these leads]. We will not let it go."

Unreliable Reports

Ironically, this debate occurred just weeks after the U.S. Supreme Court slapped down state laws that use police reports to set prison sentences because police reports are not reliable. Being on the "watch list" would also just rely on police reports. There would be no adjudication by a judge, no trial by jury, before being placed on the list. "Suspects" don't even have to be foreigners. They may have simply been individuals classified by law enforcement as sympathetic to militia groups or other undesirable domestic organizations.

Some politicians have recently experienced being on a "watch list" firsthand.

Interestingly, the same Senator Kennedy who wants to rely on "watch lists" was understandably upset [in 2004] and publicly complained to the Senate Judiciary Committee when he was prevented from flying on an airplane because his name was placed on just such a "watch list." Rules did not allow him to be told at the airport why he was being denied a ticket, but fortunately for him, being a U.S. senator meant the problem was eventually resolved with a few telephone calls.

Not the Solution

Ultimately, though, despite all the fears generated, background checks simply aren't the solution. The federal Brady Act has been in effect [since 1994] and state background checks even longer. But despite all the academic research that has been done, a National Academy of Sciences report could not find any evidence—not a single published academic study—that background checks reduce any type of violent crime.

Surely, it would be nice if these regulations worked. But it's hard to believe they will be any more successful stopping terrorists. Criminals and terrorists share much in common, starting with the fact that what they are doing is illegal. In addition, terrorists are probably smarter and engage in vastly more planning than your typical criminal, thus making the rules even less likely to be successful.

People need to remind themselves that a "watch list" is only that. It is not even probable cause. If you had probable cause that these suspects had done something illegal, you could arrest them.

Ironically, during the hearing, Mr. Kennedy spent most of his question time concerned that foreign combatants held in Guantanamo were not treated by the military with the respect that the FBI uses to handle American criminals. At the same time, he believes Americans can lose their rights to own a gun without an evidentiary hearing.

Democrats may think that people on "watch lists" should be denied their rights to own a gun, but what is next? Why not just make the system much "more efficient" and simply put all people on "watch lists" directly in prison?

> *"[With 'stand your ground' laws,] if you feel threatened, you get to shoot first and ask questions never."*

"Stand Your Ground" Laws Are a License to Murder

GunGuys.com

The GunGuys.com is a public education Web site about gun control, sponsored by the Freedom States Alliance. In the following viewpoint the authors argue that new legislation known as "Stand Your Ground" laws—laws that permit homeowners who feel threatened by trespassers or burglars to shoot them without fear of prosecution—will lead to an increase in gun violence. "Stand Your Ground" laws are more appropriately known as License to Murder, the authors contend, and are unnecessary and unsafe.

As you read, consider the following questions:

1. What was Rachel Barezinsky doing when she was shot, according to sources cited by the authors?
2. What rationalization does Allen Davis give for shooting Barezinsky, according to the *Columbus Dispatch*, cited by GunGuys.com?

Gun Guys, "License to Murder Would Legalize Shooting of Teenagers," September 11, 2006. www.gunguys.com. Reproduced by permission.

3. What are some of the problems with Ohio's proposed House Bill 541, in the authors' opinion?

The Dayton [Ohio] *Daily News* has a column up about Allen Davis, who lived in a house the neighborhood kids called haunted. One of the kids, 17-year-old Rachel Barezinsky, took a few steps onto the property with her friends, and for her trouble, Davis shot her. Currently, he's being charged with assault, but under the NRA's [National Rifle Association] new License to Murder law, Davis would be completely immune from prosecution.

It's hard not to focus on the state of Allen Davis' yard.

It seems irrelevant, but in another way it strikes at the heart of the matter.

Davis is the Worthington man so obsessed with protecting his property that he allegedly shot at five teenage girls who apparently trespassed in a childish prank. One of them, 17-year-old Rachel Barezinsky, remains critically injured after being shot in the head.

Yet Davis kept his home in such disrepair that it earned a reputation as a "haunted house." Teens whispered among themselves, "A witch lives there," and from time to time, they dared each other to step onto the property where Davis lived with his mother, Sondra.

Police said the girls were nowhere near the house—they were, in fact, driving away—when Davis opened fire with his .22-caliber rifle. "I regret that (Barezinsky was shot)," Davis told The Columbus *Dispatch* in a jailhouse interview. "However, I would ask, why was that teenage girl engaging in delinquent behavior?"

Perceived Threat vs. Actual Threat

The girls had actually exited his property and were driving by the house one more time when Davis shot at them. They represented exactly zero threat to him—and yet he fired on them

'Stand Your Ground' Measures

Twenty-one states are considering legislation that permits people to defend themselves with deadly force when they perceive life-threatening situations, even in public places. Florida enacted this law last year.

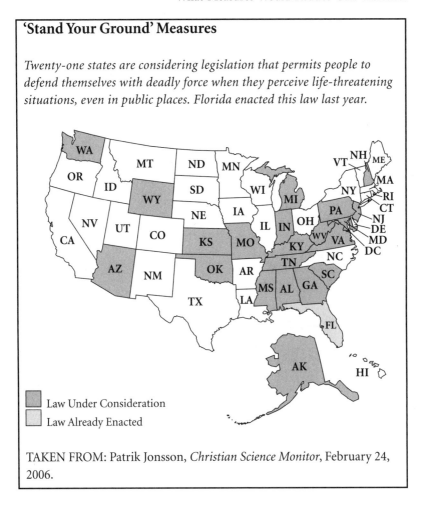

Law Under Consideration

Law Already Enacted

TAKEN FROM: Patrik Jonsson, *Christian Science Monitor*, February 24, 2006.

as if they were breaking in the door and wielding Uzis. That's an important point, because the NRA's latest legal endeavor, License to Murder, relies on percieved threat, not actual threat. Right now, Davis thinks the girls are a threat, shoots them, and is charged with assault. But License to Murder says if you feel threatened, you get to shoot first and ask questions never. Davis' perceived threat would make this crazy shooting legal.

For Toby Hoover, director of Ohio Coalition Against Gun Violence, the tragic incident speaks volumes about the world in which our children are growing up. "Forty years ago, someone might have called your mother," she said. "Now they want to shoot you."

Hoover consoles herself with the knowledge that Davis is sitting in a Franklin County jail, charged with five counts of felonious assault. But she is tormented by the thought that Ohio's proposed House Bill 541 would give people like Davis a legal defense for his actions. The bill eliminates the duty to retreat in the cases of home invasion. The bill also allows a person to use deadly force to prevent the commission of a "forcible felony"—a term that is not defined in Ohio code, Hoover notes.

"I'm afraid this bill would absolutely make Mr. Davis' actions legal," she says.

Vague Language

The bill is filled with vague language—because that's the way the NRA wants it. They want to stretch the terms as far as possible, to make using a gun as legal as they can. In essence, their bill ends up as an incitement to violence. "Go ahead and shoot," the NRA wants to say, "we'll make sure you get away with it."

But the bill's wording is murky enough to raise concerns: What constitutes "reasonable fear" of death or bodily harm? Is it the high school prankster toilet-papering your trees? The Avon Lady? The foreign exchange student?

When are we entitled to be afraid—when someone doesn't look like us, or doesn't act like us, or isn't the same age, race or economic class?

And then there's the biggest question of all: Have we become so obsessed with protecting our property that we're endangering our most precious resource of all?

"These are our children, and our first responsibility in this country is to make sure our kids are safe," Hoover says. "I'm tired of hearing about all these guys and their gun rights. What about this little girl and her rights?"

It's crystal clear that License to Murder is unnecessary and unsafe. These teens may have made a mistake in stepping onto this guy's property, but they did not deserve to be shot over it. And yet the NRA's law would let exactly that happen, completely legally.

> *"['Stand your ground' laws are] nothing more than some common-sense protections for crime victims."*

"Stand Your Ground" Laws Will Protect Crime Victims

David Kopel

"Stand Your Ground" laws expand a victim's right of self-defense against violent attackers, argues David Kopel in the following viewpoint. A victim may use deadly force against someone who unlawfully enters a person's home or vehicle, or attempts to force someone from his or her home or vehicle, Kopel asserts. This allows the victim to protect herself without fearing that her actions will be second-guessed by the prosecutor. "Stand Your Ground" laws are nothing more than common-sense protections for crime victims. Kopel, a policy analyst at the Cato Institute and research director at the Independence Institute, is an expert on firearms policy, juvenile crime, and drug policy.

As you read, consider the following questions:

1. What is the "shall issue" legislation, and how prevalent is it, according to Kopel?

David Kopel, "Florida's New Self-Defense Law," May 19, 2005. http://volokh.com/ar chives/archive_2005_05_15-2005_05_21.shtml. Reproduced by permission of the author.

2. What are some of the exceptions for when deadly force may be used, as cited by Kopel?

3. When may police arrest someone who used deadly force in self-defense, according to the author?

Florida Governor Jeb Bush signed Senate Bill 436, which expands and clarifies Floridians' self-defense rights against violent attackers. The bill was the creation of former NRA [National Rifle Association] President Marion Hammer, who is also head of Unified Sportsmen of Florida, the state's major pro-gun group. The NRA has announced that it plans to take SB 436 national and urge other states to adopt similar measures.

Previous Florida programs created by Marion Hammer have done very well in other states. In 1988, her lobbying led Florida to enact "Shall Issue" concealed handgun licensing legislation—so that any law-abiding adult with a clean record and who passes a safety training class may obtain a permit to carry a handgun for lawful protection. Before 1988, only a handful of states had Shall Issue laws; now, only a little more than a dozen states do not have such laws.

Similarly, Hammer invented the "Eddie Eagle" gun safety program, which trains elementary school–age children not to touch a gun unless they are being supervised by a responsible adult. Eddie Eagle has been taught to millions of children, has won an award from the National Safety Council, and has been lauded by state legislatures and city councils all over America.

Self-Defense Rights

So Florida-style self-defense rights may be coming to your state soon. Opponents of the law have made dire predictions about turning Florida into "the Wild West." Similar predictions were made about the Shall Issue law, and those predictions did not come true. If you read the actual text of the Florida law, it becomes clear that the new law simply codifies common-sense principles of self-defense, including the principle that violent criminals, not innocent victims, should be the ones at risk during a violent crime. . . .

A person may use deadly force against someone who unlawfully and forcefully enters a person's home or vehicle. A victim may also use deadly force against a criminal who attempts to force a person out of her vehicle or home. Thus, if someone kicks down your front door in the middle of the night, or attempts to carjack you, you can use a firearm or other deadly weapon to protect yourself. You do not have to worry that a prosecutor might second-guess your decision, and claim that you should have used lesser force against the violent intruder.

Exceptions to the Law

The bill makes several exceptions. The right to use deadly force does not apply against someone who has a right to be in the home or car (unless the person is the subject of a domestic violence restraining order or a no-contact order). The right does not apply in child custody disputes. Of course the right does not apply if the person trying to enter the home or automobile is an identified police officer acting within the scope of his duties. Similarly, persons who are using the automobile or dwelling to commit a crime are not covered. . . .

Prior Florida law about self-defense allowed defensive deadly force only when the victim believed that no lesser force would suffice. The principle remains in effect in all self-defense situations in Florida, except when the attack takes place in the home or automobile; the legislative judgment was that attacks in a home or vehicle are so outrageous, and so threatening to the social order, that victims should be guaranteed that they will be protected from having their defensive decisions second-guessed in court.

The Castle Doctrine

That's what this law is all about: restoring your right under the Castle Doctrine [the right to use force to protect one's home and property] and the Constitution to protect yourself, your family and others. Your home is your castle, and you have a right—as ancient as time itself—to absolute safety in it.

Marion P. Hammer, Atlanta Journal-Constitution,
May 2, 2005.

Victims Are Not Required to Retreat

Outside of the home or vehicle, a victim may only use deadly force when it is reasonably believed to be necessary. (So the victim continues to face a risk of prosecutorial second-guessing). However, the new law specifies that victims are not legally obliged to retreat anywhere:

> A person who is not engaged in an unlawful activity and who is attacked in any other place where he or she has a right to be has no duty to retreat and has the right to stand his or her ground and meet force with force, including deadly force if he or she reasonably believes it is necessary to do so to prevent death or great bodily harm to himself or herself or another or to prevent the commission of a forcible felony.

So if a gang tries to mug you while you are walking down a dark street, and you draw a gun and shoot one of the gangsters, a prosecutor cannot argue that you should have tried to run away. The prosecutor still can, however, argue that use of deadly force was unnecessary, because the victim could have used lesser force in the particular situation.

Other Provisions of the Law

The next section of the law makes explicit one of the presumptions of the law—that violent invaders of the home or automobile are presumed to be intending to commit violent crimes after they enter.

> A person who unlawfully and by force enters or attempts to enter a person's dwelling, residence, or occupied vehicle is presumed to be doing so with the intent to commit an unlawful act involving force or violence. . . .

The final section of the bill prohibits tort lawsuits against persons who act in conformity with the law. A criminal who sues a crime victim will be liable for the victim's legal expenses. Police officers are not allowed to arrest a victim who defended herself, unless the officers have probable cause to believe the victim violated the laws. . . .

Common-Sense Protections

Principled opponents of the Florida law can object to the bill because it allows deadly force against home invaders and carjackers, because crime victims are not required to retreat, or because criminals may not sue crime victims. In the United Kingdom, such objections would carry the day. [In 2006], the Blair government defeated a move in Parliament to ease Britain's severe restrictions on self-defense in the home, because, in the British government's view, criminals also have a right to be protected against violence. Likewise, the British courts have allowed burglars to sue victims who used force against them.

But in the United States, social attitudes tend to favor the victim's rights over those of the criminal. Most Americans would disagree with the idea that a mugging victim should be sent to prison because he didn't try to flee, or that violent predators ought to be able to sue victims who shoot them.

As the Florida bill is introduced in other states, victims-rights opponents will probably be successful in getting newspapers and television to describe the proposal in very frightening terms. But when legislators and their aides read the actual text of the bill, many legislators will—like their Florida counterparts—conclude that bill is nothing more than some common-sense protections for crime victims.

Periodical Bibliography

The following articles have been selected to supplement the diverse views presented in this chapter.

Tom Avril — "'Smart Gun' Shows Promise and Promises Controversy," *Philadelphia Inquirer*, May 29, 2006.

Mark Benjamin — "Tough on Terror, Weak on Guns," *Salon*, March 28, 2005. www.salon.com.

Anthony A. Braga and Glenn L. Pierce — "Disrupting Illegal Firearms Markets in Boston: The Effects of Operation Ceasefire on the Supply of New Handguns to Criminals," *Criminology*, November 2005.

Michelle Cottle — "Shoot First, Regret Legislation Later," *Time*, May 9, 2005.

Fred Grimm — "New Law Gives Too Many People a License to Kill," *Miami* (FL) *Herald*, August 24, 2006.

Patrik Jonsson — "Is Self-Defense Law Vigilante Justice?" *Christian Science Monitor*, February 26, 2006.

John R. Lott Jr. — "If Gun Background Checks Don't Work, Will 'Watch Lists' Be Any More Effective?" *Investor's Business Daily*, March 22, 2005.

New York Times — "Guns for Terrorists," April 4, 2005.

New York Times — "Shoot First—No Questions Asked," August 14, 2006.

Tom Perrotta — "City Wins Bid to Sue Manufacturers over Marketing of Weapons," *New York Law Journal*, December 5, 2005.

Richard D. Vogel — "Florida's 'Stand Your Ground' Law: Killing in Defense of Private Property, at Home or in the Streeets," *Monthly Review*, April 10, 2005.

For Further Discussion

Chapter 1

1. Jane E. Brody and Wayne LaPierre discuss the heartbreak of gun deaths among children. They both agree that the deaths of children due to guns is undeniably tragic, but they differ in their perspectives of how pervasive gun deaths are among children. Compare and contrast their arguments; in what ways are their arguments similar? How do they differ?

2. Michael Caswell asserts that banning "assault weapons" will not lower crime rates, because criminals will simply find another weapon to use to commit their crime. Do you agree with him that Americans should have the right to own assault weapons? Why or why not?

3. Based on your readings of the viewpoints in this chapter by Michael Huemer and Adam Lichtenheld, do you think concealed-weapons laws increase or decrease levels of gun violence? In your opinion, should private citizens be permitted to carry concealed weapons? Explain your answer citing data from the viewpoints.

Chapter 2

1. The Legal Action Project maintains that the right to keep and bear arms is a collective right reserved for state militias. Robert A. Levy, on the other hand, argues that gun ownership is an individual right. What evidence do the authors present to support their arguments? In your opinion, how should the Second Amendment be interpreted? Defend your answer, using examples from the viewpoints.

2. Jason Kallini asserts that any restrictions on gun usage and ownership infringes the right to keep and bear arms

and is therefore unconstitutional. Saul Cornell contends that gun ownership has been regulated since the time of the Founding Fathers, and therefore gun control is not only constitutional, but required. Based on your reading of the viewpoints, do you think individual gun ownership can be legally restricted? Why or why not?

Chapter 3

1. Many of the authors in this anthology discuss the possible threats to U.S. security if terrorists were to use .50-caliber rifles in their attacks. Based on your readings of the viewpoints, do you think .50-caliber rifles should be banned? Why or why not? Support your answer with examples from the viewpoints.

2. John Moorhouse and Ik-Whan G. Kwon and Daniel W. Baack come to opposite conclusions about whether crime rates in states with strong gun control laws are affected by weak gun control laws in neighboring states. Which argument do you find more persuasive? Why?

Chapter 4

1. The organization Americans for Gun Safety claims there is a loophole in the regulations governing gun shows that allows guns to be sold without requiring gun buyers to undergo a background check. Orrin G. Hatch maintains that the rules for selling guns at a gun show are the same whether the gun is sold by a gun dealer or a private individual. Based on your readings of the viewpoints in this anthology, should every gun buyer at a gun show be subject to a background check regardless of whether the gun seller is a licensed firearm dealer or a private seller? Why or why not? Support your answer with examples from the viewpoints.

2. Steven E. Roberts and John R. Lott Jr. and Sonya D. Jones disagree on whether people on a terrorist watch list

should be permitted to buy firearms. In your opinion, is such a restriction constitutionally permissible? Explain your answer.

3. Based on your readings of the viewpoints in this anthology, will "Stand Your Ground" laws that allow crime victims to shoot their attackers if they feel threatened without fear of prosecution lead to an increase in gun violence, or are they necessary to protect a victim's right to defend himself or herself against violent attackers? Support your answer with examples from the viewpoints.

4. Gun control proponents advocate a number of measures to reduce gun violence, such as waiting periods, background checks, licensing and registration of handguns, trigger locks, ammunition fingerprinting, and even banning certain weapons. Opponents of gun control contend that any restrictions on firearms and gun ownership are unconstitutional and would be ineffective in reducing gun-related crime. In your opinion, what measures, if any, do you think should be imposed on guns, ammunition, and gun buyers and sellers? Explain your answer.

Organizations to Contact

American Civil Liberties Union
125 Broad St., 18th Fl., New York, NY   10004
(212) 944-9800 • fax: (212) 869-9065
Web site: www.aclu.org

The ACLU is an organization that works to defend the rights and principles delineated in the Declaration of Independence and the U.S. Constitution. It champions the "collective" interpretation of the Second Amendment; in other words, it believes that the Second Amendment does not guarantee the individual right to own and bear firearms. Consequently, the organization believes that gun control is constitutional and necessary in some situations. The ACLU publishes the semiannual *Civil Liberties* in addition to policy statements and reports.

Americans for Gun Safety (AGS)
Washington, DC
(202) 775-0300 • fax: (202) 775-0430
www.americansforgunsafety.com

Americans for Gun Safety seeks to promote responsible gun ownership and to educate Americans on existing gun laws and new policy options for reducing access to guns by criminals and children. Through legislative measures and public outreach, AGS supports the rights of law-abiding gun owners and promotes reasonable and effective proposals for fighting gun crime. AGS provides background, research, and reference materials to the public and to policy makers on issues relating to gun safety.

Brady Center to Prevent Gun Violence
1250 Eye St. NW, Suite 1100, Washington, DC   20005
(202) 289-7319 • fax: (202) 408-1851
Web site: www.bradycenter.org

The Brady Center is the largest national nonpartisan grass-roots organization leading the fight to prevent gun violence. It works to enact and enforce sensible gun laws, regulations, and public policies through grassroots activism, electing pro–gun control public officials and increasing public awareness of gun violence. The Brady Center also works to reform the gun industry and educate the public about gun violence through litigation and grassroots mobilization. Various reports and press releases are available on its Web site.

Cato Institute
1000 Massachusetts Ave. NW, Washington, DC   20001
(202) 842-0200 • fax: (202) 842-3290
Web site: www.cato.org

The Cato Institute is a libertarian public-policy research foundation. It evaluates government policies and offers reform proposals and commentary on its Web site. Its publications include the Cato Policy Analysis series of reports, which have covered topics such as "Fighting Back: Crime, Self-Defense, and the Right to Carry a Handgun," and "Trust the People: The Case Against Gun Control." It also publishes the magazine *Regulation*, the *Cato Policy Report*, and numerous book-length studies.

Citizens Committee for the Right to Keep and Bear Arms
12500 NE Tenth Pl., Bellevue, WA   98005
(425) 454-4911 • fax: (425) 451-3959
e-mail: info@ccrkba.org
Web site: www.ccrkba.org

The committee believes that the U.S. Constitution's Second Amendment guarantees and protects the right of individual Americans to own guns. It works to educate the public concerning this right and to lobby legislators to prevent the passage of gun control laws. The committee is affiliated with the Second Amendment Foundation. It distributes the books *Gun Laws of America, Gun Rights Fact Book, Origin of the Second Amendment,* and *Point Blank: Guns and Violence in America.*

Coalition to Stop Gun Violence
1000 Sixteenth St. NW, Suite 603
Washington, DC   20036-5705
(202) 530-0340 • fax: (202) 530-0331
e-mail: noguns@aol.com
Web site: www.gunfree.org

The Coalition to Stop Gun Violence lobbies at the local, state, and federal levels to ban the sale of handguns and assault weapons to individuals and to institute licensing and registration of all firearms. It also litigates cases against firearm makers. Its publications include various informational sheets on gun violence and the *Annual Citizens' Conference to Stop Gun Violence Briefing Book*, a compendium of gun control fact sheets, arguments, and resources.

Independence Institute
14142 Denver West Pkwy., Suite 101, Golden, CO   80401
(303) 279-6536 • fax: (303) 279-4176
Web site: www.i2i.org

The Independence Institute is a pro–free market think tank that supports gun ownership as a civil liberty and a constitutional right. Its publications include booklets opposing gun control, such as *Children and Guns: Sensible Solutions,* "*Shall Issue": The New Wave of Concealed Handgun Permit Laws,* and *Unfair and Unconstitutional: The New Federal Gun Control and Juvenile Crime Proposals,* as well as the book *Guns: Who Should Have Them?* Its Web site also contains articles, fact sheets, and commentary from a variety of sources.

Jews for the Preservation of Firearms Ownership (JPFO)
PO Box 270143, Hartford, WI   53207
(262) 673-9745 • fax: (262) 673-9746
e-mail: jpfo@jpfo.org
Web site: www.jpfo.org

JPFO is an educational organization that believes Jewish law mandates self-defense. Its primary goal is the elimination of the idea that gun control is a socially useful public policy in any country. JPFO publishes the quarterly *Firearms Sentinel*, the booklet *Will 'Gun Control' Make You Safer?* and regular news alerts.

National Crime Prevention Council (NCPC)

1700 K St. NW, 2nd Fl., Washington, DC   20006-3817
(202) 261-4111 • fax: (202) 296-1356
Web site: www.ncpc.org

The NCPC is a branch of the U.S. Department of Justice. It works to teach Americans how to reduce crime and addresses the causes of crime in its programs and educational materials. It provides readers with information on gun control and gun violence. The NCPC's publications include the newsletter *Catalyst*, the book *Reducing Gun Violence: What Communities Can Do*, and the booklet *Making Children, Families, and Communities Safe from Violence*.

National Firearms Association (NFA)

Box 4384, Station C, Calgary
  AB T2T 5N2
  Canada
(403) 640-1110 • fax: (403) 640-1144
Web site: www.nfa.ca

The NFA is the primary reservoir of legal and legislative expertise in the Canadian firearms community. It provides research data, expert witnesses, and education to the firearms community and others. NFA publishes the monthly newsletter *Pointblank* as well as *Canadian Hunting & Shooting, Bowhunting*, and *Angler* magazines.

National Institute of Justice (NIJ)

Box 6000, Rockville, MD   20849
(301) 519-5500
Web site: www.ncjrs.org

A component of the Office of Justice Programs of the U.S. Department of Justice, the NIJ supports research on crime, criminal behavior, and crime prevention. The National Criminal Justice Reference Service acts as a clearinghouse that provides information and research about criminal justice. Its publications include the research briefs "Reducing Youth Gun Violence: An Overview of Programs and Initiatives," "Impacts of the 1994 Assault Weapons Ban," and "Homicide in Eight U.S. Cities: Trends, Context, and Policy Implications."

National Rifle Association (NRA)
11250 Waples Mill Rd., Fairfax, VA   22030
(703) 267-1000 • fax: (703) 267-3989
Web site: www.nra.org

The NRA is America's largest organization of gun owners. It is the primary lobbying group for those who oppose gun control laws. The NRA believes that such laws violate the U.S. Constitution and do nothing to reduce crime. In addition to its monthly magazines *American Rifleman, American Hunter,* and *Incites,* the NRA publishes numerous books, bibliographies, reports, and pamphlets on gun ownership, gun safety, and gun control.

Second Amendment Foundation
12500 NE Tenth Pl., Bellevue, WA   98005
(206) 454-7012 • fax: (206) 451-3959
Web site: www.saf.org

The foundation is dedicated to informing Americans about their Second Amendment right to keep and bear firearms. It believes that gun control laws violate this right. The foundation publishes numerous books, including *The Amazing Vanishing Second Amendment, The Best Defense: True Stories of Intended Victims Who Defended Themselves with a Firearm,* and *CCW: Carrying Concealed Weapons.* The complete text of the book *How to Defend Your Gun Rights* is available on its Web site.

Violence Policy Center
2000 P St. NW, Suite 200, Washington, DC   20036

(202) 822-8200 • fax: (202) 822-8202
Web site: www.vpc.org

The center is an educational foundation that conducts research on firearms violence. It works to educate the public
concerning the dangers of guns and supports gun control
measures. The center's publications include the report *Handgun Licensing and Registration: What It Can and Cannot Do,
GUNLAND USA: A State-by-State Ranking of Gun Shows, Gun
Retailers, Machine Guns, and Gun Manufacturers,* and *Guns for
Felons: How the NRA Works to Rearm Criminals.*

Bibliography of Books

Shay Bilchik | *Reducing Youth Gun Violence: An Overview of Programs and Initiatives Program Report*. Collingdale, PA: Diane, 2004.

Sarah Brady | *A Good Fight*. New York: PublicAffairs, 2002.

Gregg Lee Carter | *Guns in American Society: An Encyclopedia of History, Politics, Culture, and the Law*. Santa Barbara, CA: ABC-CLIO, 2002.

Saul Cornell | *A Well-Regulated Militia: The Founding Fathers and the Origins of Gun Control*. New York: Oxford University Press, 2006.

Constance Emerson Crooker | *Gun Control and Gun Rights*. Westport, CT: Greenwood, 2003.

Wendy Cukier and Victor W. Sidel | *The Global Gun Epidemic: From Saturday Night Specials to AK-47s*. Westport, CT: Praeger, 2006.

Alexander Deconde | *Gun Violence in America: The Struggle for Control*. Boston: Northeastern University Press, 2003.

Susan Dudley Gold | *Gun Control*. New York: Benchmark, 2004.

Bernard E. Harcourt | *Language of the Gun: Youth, Crime, and Public Policy*. Chicago: University of Chicago Press, 2006.

David Hemenway   *Private Guns, Public Health*. Ann Arbor: University of Michigan Press, 2004.

Harry Henderson   *Gun Control*. New York: Facts On File, 2005.

Caitlin Kelly   *Blown Away: American Women and Guns*. New York: Pocket, 2004.

David M. Kennedy, Anthony A. Braga, and Anne M. Piehl   *Reducing Gun Violence: The Boston Project's Operation Ceasefire*. Collingdale, PA: Diane, 2004.

Gary Kleck   *Point Blank: Guns and Violence in America*. New York: Aldine de Gruyter, 2005.

Wayne LaPierre   *The Global War on Your Guns: Inside the U.N. Plan to Destroy the Bill of Rights*. Nashville: Nelson Current, 2006.

Wayne LaPierre   *Guns, Freedom and Terrorism*. Nashville: WND Books, 2003.

Wayne LaPierre   *Shooting Straight: Telling the Truth About Guns in America*. Washington, DC: Regnery, 2002.

John R. Lott Jr.   *The Bias Against Guns*. Washington, DC: Regnery, 2003.

Joyce Lee Malcolm   *Guns and Violence: The English Experience*. Cambridge, MA: Harvard University Press, 2002.

Melody Maysonet, ed. — *NRA: An American Legend.* Ft. Lauderdale, FL: Write Stuff Enterprises, 2002.

Jack Reynolds — *A People Armed and Free: The Truth About the Second Amendment.* Bloomington, IN: First Books, 2003.

Robert J. Spitzer — *The Politics of Gun Control.* 3rd ed. Washington, DC: CQ Press, 2004.

Charles Fruehling Springwood — *Open Fire: Understanding Global Gun Cultures.* New York: Berg, 2007.

Carol X. Vinzant — *Lawyers, Guns, and Money: One Man's Battle with the Gun Industry.* New York: Palgrave Macmillan, 2005.

David C. Williams — *The Mythic Meanings of the Second Amendment: Taming Political Violence in a Constitutional Republic.* New Haven, CT: Yale University Press, 2003.

Geraldine Woods — *Right to Bear Arms.* New York: Facts On File, 2005.

Index